BECOMING BALANCED:

For those of you who, like me, have exhausted every rationalised and offered understanding of life.

In Loving Memory of A.c.M
And with special thanks and all my love to the one consistently caring and supportive relative I ever had, Mum.

◆ ◆ ◆

Foreword.

The refreshing chill of the leather on this chair and the background base from the speaker continuously providing creative comfort is about as joyous as the completion of this book. Through the book I look through the mess and complex growth spirts I've taken to get here. I'm left with a deeper sense of being in the moment. The anxiety and un answered questions have been put to rest for me through this experience. I urge anyone feeling at an impass in life to make peace with the past and become balanced before tackling your next mission. As I mention in the book, lifes always changing and even since finishing these pages I'm in a different mindset about it,I could adapt and change it for the rest of my life but that would take away the authenticity. Its raw and real and flawed and thats perfect, because thats what lifes really like.

If this is your first introduction to any of my work, this is the best place to start.The mindset and outlooks I have developed through life have lead me to starting my company Balanced Dreamers. This book is about where those teachings came from for me and why I would die behind the ethos. I don't believe your truly successful or happy until you find your balance in life. Whatever that means for you. In this human experience we find ourselves in its easy to escape into comfort and stagnation from fear and learned habits. This book isn't to kick you into action or guilt you into working harder. It's to find a place within yourself, your stable foundation that is unshakeable through whatever life chooses to throw at you. From there everything becomes not just a lesson or a struggle forward but a joyous existence no matter where you find yourself.

Why did I write this book?
Even now in 2020, 84 young men loose their lifes to suicide. Depression, addiction and mental illness being at the core of almost all of them. Where I live no one talked abot mental health apart from my mum who was a counsellor and almost devoted completely to it. I feel it needs to be as normal and as much in everyday life as coffee in the mornings. The truth is its not spoken about enough, its not funded enough and its not good enough at the moment. We should never have to loose a life from suicide, life is your greatest gift it needs to be celebrated and nurtured as such. This book will be used to grow awareness of mental health and health in general. I'm holding my hands up and telling you it was nearly myself in their shoes. Therefore my story and vulnerabilities are the least I can offer to help another deal with theirs. Im also holding my hands up and admitting I don't have all the answers amd I don't have the power or financies to change the world right now but this is a start. If everyone cultivated love and joy and healthy progression into their lives and spoke about their shortcomings the world becomes a more balanced abundant peaceful place.

For me to look around and realise that everything around me was once exactly what I wanted it caused me to pause. For one reason I didn't fully remember how I had got here, it felt as though just yesterday I was someone who was on a downward spiral into addiction, depression and chaos. I wanted to make sure I knew what had changed I wanted to grasp it and give it to others. For the most part I just had to get it off my chest. If your like me then the amount of thoughts I go through even on a single day are powerful enough to change who I am completely. The learning curve I had been on for the last twenty five years had been a painful blur and if I could make someone elses journey less painful it would be worth the effort.

I also see it as planting roots for Balanced, to carve out the ethos that runs through the book and the community I'm building. I wanted you all to feel as though you went through it with me. I want to know your stories and what's worked for you, I want a world for my son to grow up in where strangers look out for one another and unneccessary suffering is irradicated. Where health and joy is the new success. Where the so painfully longed after balance returns to this chaotic magical unfathomable world we find ourselves in.

BECOMING BALANCED

My hope of writing this is not to give a play by play of what happened in my life, but to try and illustrate the changes that I went through over the years. Along with being explorational for myself, as I want to see where I've developed some of my habits and see if there are any patterns in which I can change to improve myself. I hope, that for other people, reading this may help them, to see where I came from through the uncomfortable and unavoidable growth that naturally occurs and ultimately why I am who I am. Maybe others can learn from my experience or recognise their own journeys lessons. This won't necessarily be a complete timeline, its more whatever comes up for me and things I value and remember most about my past. The events and changes I feel have led to growth as a person. How I overcame the struggles and hurdles on my path. I don't claim to have had an extremely hard life or think the hurdles I've overcame are anything more severe than anyone else, but the emotional and physical stress and discomfort is real, for everyone's situation. Hopefully this book will help others to realise that no matter how small and insignificant your problems can seem in relevence to the magnitude of the rest of the worlds issues, it can have the same internal impact on our emotions and mental wellbeing, and that in itself shouldn't be diminished or brushed off as being less of a man, or human.I say man because for as long as I've been living there has always been a stigma around mental health for men, especially in western scotland. Its never spoke about and when it is it's quickly brushed under the carpet with humour and disconnect.My aim is to show that the power you give these areas in your life ultimately determines how well you'll cope with the adversities life will inevitably throw at you. Lastly to show my overriding belief around balance and how it has grown to be my most powerful mental asset and often, throughout my life, been my last strand of hope.

I was born 26th of June 1995 by my mother Tracy, son to my dad Alistair and younger brother to David, this immediate family is the most love and security and "family" I've ever known. I say "family" because there are more relations that come in and out of my story with lessons and implications along the way, but we'll get to that. We lived in a big Victorian style house with high ceilings and traditionally decorated ceiling cornice's and the extravagant ceiling rose with chandeliers hanging tastefully from both living rooms. Floor to ceiling windows naturally lit the home, leaving it cool in summer and cosy in the winter when the coal fires were on. We also had what we called the "cold store" that was a room next to the kitchen with a stone floor. It was an original cold room used as a fridge before fridges were invented. We now used to cool dads beer and keep our shoes in. For almost every meal of my childhood we sat at the table as a family the kitchen was always the family hub to me. Out the back of our beautiful home was a not so beautiful plot of waste ground. The owner had planted thousands of trees and bushes and then left for South Africa over twenty years ago. What remained was a wild unkempt small forrest, that we called the plant-in. Along with the trees you would often find birds, foxes, fly tipping points and the odd teenagers sharing a can of cider or two. Who am I kidding it was usually buckfast, this was Scotland right enough. We had tried to get planning permission to create a small garden from the grounds, but solicitors couldn't find or contact the owner.We eventually took it into our own hands and made the garden ourselves. It took us weeks, clearing out bushes and tree stumps with only manual tools and sheers then painstakingly levelling the ground. We worked as a team just the four of us, me and my brother were not old enough to do all the heavy lifting and my dad was in his mid-fifties, although remarkably fit for his age. We all had to chip in, it was my first experience with hard work and equally accomplishment,taking it from this overgrown mess of trees and branches, and with our own hands made a lovely back garden. A space to spend time with family in what little sun we got,with the newly painted fence and old stone wall.

Other than a vague image of 3 year old me running across a field in a bright yellow jacket my earliest memories all included our family dog. She's in the background of all my childhood memories, either sitting under my chair at the dinner table, as I always fed her from my plate when my parents weren't looking. Or sitting with her head poking out the gate at the front of the house for hour's people watching and receiving her share of ear scratches and admiration from those passing by.Her name was Teddy named solely because she looked just like a teddy, her jet black saddle of fur gracefully fitting with the golden brown that covered her face legs and tail, she had been the runt of the litter but through our nurturing feeding and care had grown into a stunning specimen of her breed. She was my best friend growing up at times as dogs are to a lot of young boys. Later she would unfortunately be my first experience with death but many good memories were between then and now. When I was getting in to trouble as a child I would go sit with the dog for a while with my pouted lip, she always knew how to cheer me up. I have very fond memories of the early days in our home.

The town, however, this beautiful home was planted in wasn't the prettiest, like all places there's the areas where poverty and crime are a daily part of life. Often rubbing shoulders with successful families without too much friction. We weren't overly wealthy as a family, we had a big house but the income wasn't extravagant and as time passed and new houses were built and the car stopped being upgraded each year we were just above working class, if I had to label it. I remember we had this old red rover car that we ran into the ground before we eventually got a new one .It was a joke amongst us that the rust and dirt was the only thing keeping it together. Although I think they could have got a new one sooner my mum and dad were not flashy or materialistic at all. They had both came from a lot less than they had and they worked hard to give me and my brother a different lifestyle to that of their own upbringing, and for that I can't fault them. It wasn't until later in life as I look back I remember seeing stress from my mum and dad around money. Not realising the jobs my mum had been doing were not only so she could continue her education, but to help keep the roof over our heads. No matter how they were struggling they never let it show to me, I never went without anything and I trusted fully that we were financially stable.

My big brother was two years older than me, and he elevated a lot of the stress going into nursery and school as he'd been there before me and told me what to expect. Going into nursery I just felt like it was a big playtime just making friends and doing as they told me. I had begun hurting myself a lot though, not intentionally, I needed glasses but we never realised until after I had ran into the pillars at nursery a couple times, on the same day. I was rarely without a black eye or a burst nose, not that I let it slow me down. Getting glasses and going for the eye tests didn't bother me at that age, my dad wore glasses and the social aspect of life hadn't really addressed self-image yet. It wasn't until I moved into primary 1 that I became self-conscious about wearing them, when I saw I was different. Although I tried to keep them off to blend in, I was encouraged to wear them from the teachers and my parents, as there was the potential my eyesight would improve to where I didn't need to wear them anymore, thankfully that's exactly what happened. Just before leaving primary school, I was told my eye sight had improved enough to where I only had to wear them when reading or playing playstation. I remember asking my dad to run my newly retired glasses over in the car.

Home life at this point was pretty standard my mum worked with my dad at a dental laboratory making crowns and veneers, I'd later work alongside my dad in this field briefly. My dad progressed to manager of the lab shortly after I had started school. This gave my mum a bit more freedom to go and pursue her dream of becoming a psychotherapist, which she has been now for over 20 years now and has excelled to become considered an expert by her peers, appearing on radio to speak on grief and being asked to speak infront of aspiring counsellors and peers. She now spends her working life training new counsellors and passing on her experiences, a job I feel fits her perfectly . But during her journey there were times she had to work menial jobs that clearly caused her some stress and discomfort. She would do care in the community with the local care homes, as it was part of her counselling training to do a certain amount of hours of volunteer work to gain experience,and she would also work in the local bakers to make extra money.

At this age and very little understanding of life I didn't realise there was anything different about our family, they were all I knew and felt I ever needed. As I got older and more aware I started seeing other people's dads and realised mine was a lot older than most other boys my age. My dad was 20 years older than my mum making him in his late fifties before I ever started school. It didn't bother me or my brother he was just our dad, all we'd ever known. Later though I can see that his age did have some implications on me albeit that of a positive effect. In my pursuits of building strength and muscle, I believe it had something to do with seeing my dad as small and weaker than the younger dads we saw at school. He had worked at a desk for over 30 years at this point and his back was slowly beginning to arch over. Despite his health being remarkable as he aged he was, to put it as polite as possible, past his prime physically before I was born. I was born 4 days before my dad's 50th birthday, I was his present and I feel it's why we did grow to be so close.

At home I had my big brother for entertainment, we would make believe games and wrestle and fight like all children did, he was the best big brother though because he never let me win. He is still extremely competitive and although there was two years between us he made me try harder to beat him fairly. Without meaning to he gave me that hunger to be better than I was by trying to beat him from a very young age. I was also a content child as my mother tells me I could play myself with a few toys for hours making up whole worlds with my imagination and making her laugh when I'd dress up as the characters that were in my head. Notably the time I had the belt from my mums white house coat wrapped around me like an Indian, from one of my cowboy movies, with a hobby horse and a laser shooting gun, hair spiked up running around the living room pretending to shoot them. Even at this age maybe 4-5 I was doing it not just for fun and because I could but to make my mum and dad laugh, to be a bit of a showman, I don't know where it came from but it made me feel good to see they were enjoying it as well.

Moving from nursery to primary school was the first time I experienced anxiety. I understand even babies can sense anxiousness and you can feel it early in your life, but for me I knew what it was, to an extent. I was able to understand it was something I was doing, I was making myself anxious by what I was thinking and with my mother studying counselling I knew the name of it early. I was suddenly aware that people could judge me that there was a whole world of other families out there and their opinion or outlook might be different than mine, did that mean we could be wrong? Our lifestyle and ways of being?. This was unsettling to me it opened up a whole thought process I wasn't aware of before, becoming self-conscious not only scared me it also motivated me. To be who I wanted to be not only for myself but to be that version of me for everyone else. To be the cool friend and the one people would come to. Maybe that would settle my discomfort and new found vulnerability. This encouraged me to make friends with those I wanted to be like, the athletic types the ones who didn't seem to try too hard in school but weren't the slow ones either, I played football at lunch times, as that's what they did and tried to have that universal chilled aura around me. I didn't even particularly like football, I for sure wasn't that good at it but I acted as though I liked it and played the best I could and the rest of my social life seemed to come together from there. The blunt innocence of myself at that age allowed me just not to think about the anxiety and continue to not let it change my attitude. Along with the external support from making friends and feeling part of the "norm" of school life I have mostly good memories from primary school. Academically I was consistently average, I don't remember putting in a lot of effort to stay there for the next few years at least, but I don't think I ever really gave my all to project or assignment. I was doing enough to be where I wanted to be for social reasons and for my own pride of not wanting to be at the bottom, and not a lot else.

Life continued to be routine and my mum and dad were attentive throughout homework and tests. Summer was usually spend with 2 weeks abroad all-inclusive playing in the pool with my brother and I trying to eat as much ice cream as we could get away with. My dad was the one making a case for us to go away every year, he loved travelling, having seen most of the world and travelling late into his sixties himself and with friends, but I think they suffered financially for it at times. My mum and dad had their arguments but never anything serious in front of me and my brother. Mostly their arguments had stemmed from situations with other family members, my mum didn't get on with my dad's sister. She was to put it bluntly a snobby cow, who didn't want her brother with some young gold digger as she seen it. She would use my dad's good nature and my mums will for them to get along to get them to do things for her, like helping her move and DIY jobs at her house even though she had daughters and a younger son in law she knew my dad would do it. I also remember her moving all her stuff into one of the rooms in our house while hers was being renovated. We lost a full room for weeks as she stayed with her daughter down the street. Later the feud between her and my mum would reach a point that my mum gave up on her. I was about 10 years old and passed her on the street when I got sent for the morning rolls, we called her nana, I shouted nana! Nana! A few times with only a couple meters between us but she ignored me and kept walking. I wasn't shocked or hurt by this at the time, I figured she was getting old and her hearing wasn't so good. I told my mum later about this and when she brought it up all my nana all she had to say was "you ignored my daughter". She *had* deliberately ignored me. Now my mum still looks after her mother who treated her far worse than my nana ever did and she would always put others before herself regardless of her opinions, so there was no way this was true. I began to see more clearly the dynamic in our "family". We were treated as outsiders, and I never understood why.

My dad was not very well liked by my mums side of the family either, her mother felt he was too old for her daughter and that he was just after a younger model, as it were. Despite the ridicule and judgement they received they didn't let it spoil their feelings for each other. They showed us how to keep moving forward with little support and even sabotage from people who are supposed to love them unconditionally. The more life went on the bigger picture of our family didn't paint a happy picture. I didn't care, I had the three most important people in my life under the same roof every night, everyone else would be treated as they treated me.

I remember being on the beach with my brother one summer and my dad was pretty old school so he let us go play and he walked along the elevated path that ran alongside the beach watching us. My brother and I started to dig a hole with our plastic spades and buckets. Just deep enough so our little legs at the time were dangling in as we sat on the edge, when this group of older boys came over. I remember feeling intimidated but not scared I didn't think life could touch me with my family around me, these boys tried to talk to us but we were too young to know what to say after all they were strangers. I sheepishly looked across the hole at my brother who had an expression on his face that made my heart rate increase, even at this age I was aware of how feelings could affect my physical body, despite not having the vocabulary to express it. He looked like he didn't like what was happening which made me uneasy. This was not like him. He always had and still has this confidence that's written all over his face in the most unboastful or cocky way,but at that moment he looked scared. The boys started to kick the sand back into the hole we had dug to our dismay, at this point I heard "Oi!!!" coming from the wall behind us. It put shivers down my back, I turned to see my dad who was usually a very peaceful gentleman, a man who until now I had never seen being aggressive in the slightest, jump from that wall as if it was nothing. I don't know how high the wall was but to my years it felt like he was going to hurt himself on the landing. After a super hero-like landing he was over at that hole in seconds kicking sand and chasing this group of about 4 or 5 boys away shouting something along the lines of "get to fuck away from my boys". They of course dispersed immediately.

Once the initial shock had gone for me and my brother it went back to normal but I never looked at my dad as just this friendly older guy again, I was so proud he was my dad. Walking back to the car that day I had got tired so he was carrying me, just as we got to the car the same group of boys from the beach were waiting near the car. The oldest one in his full kappa tracksuit piped up and said something about my dad getting sand in his little brothers eye and that he was going to get his dad etc., with the rest of them trying to look as menacing as possible behind him. My dad never said anything as far as I remember even with me asking him "what we going to do dad?, he calmly put us in the car made sure the seatbelts were secure and drove off, as if they weren't there. He obviously seen them for what they were, just young boys, he had nothing to prove by being aggressive or violent he wasn't phased by it.

My dad had grown up in Glasgow just after the Second World War, he had a twin brother an older brother and sister in a small flat near Yorkhill hospital. The stories he told me about growing up stay with me to this day and although I spent most of my life with him there was always new stories to be told about his life. His mum died when he was 13 and his dad worked all day so the boys had free rein essentially, they got into trouble as you can imagine including being in court twice in the same day at 14 for playing football on the street and I quote "walking on the grass". Not exactly the Kray twins childhood but he was far from a push over, he wasn't exactly fearful either. Him and his twin brother were once picked up by the coastguard for taking an inflatable dingy down the River Clyde not for the faint of heart for a strong swimmer but my dad and his brother couldn't swim a stroke. Even growing up on our family holidays he barely ever got in the water and if he did it was just deep enough so his feet comfortably reached the ground. He would later speak to me about protecting myself when I picked up boxing and other martial arts. He never spoke fondly of violence having grown up when the knife crime was at an all time high in Glasgow but he would teach me how to throw a punch and when to walk away. He told me never to raise my hands unless I was prepared to use them. Meaning I would need to be prepared to face the consequences that came with that.

My mum grew up in Clydebank, with a mother who I can only imagine was worse than being in foster care. She was horrible to my mum throughout her life, my mum cooked and cleaned the house done everything herself and was verbally and on occasion physically abused by her mum whenever she was in a bad mood, which is constantly as far as I know her. Her dad was her favourite, he was in the navy, she always spoke very highly of her dad and that I was very like him. He unfortunately wasn't there a lot because of his work in the navy leaving my mum with her unsavoury mother and her big brother,who despite being older and a big guy at over 6foot 7 took his fair share of abuse and unwarranted discipline from my 5 foot nothing gran. I never got to meet my grandad from my mum's side as he sadly passed away while on holiday at only 50 years old, my mum was 20 at the time. My mum tells me of how she had had a dream the night before he died,where she was trying to comfort her mum. Who in the dream was sat on the floor in front of the couch crying, as much as she tried my mum couldn't get to her to comfort her. Which to me might have something to do with the resentment she must have felt for her. It doesn't surprise me but it does say a lot about the type of person my mum is, even after how horribly her mother treated her she still tried to comfort her in her dream. She went on to tell me that one night after her mum had returned from the holiday she did find her in the same spot from her dream and comforted her. I do believe in a higher power as there have been situations like this throughout my life that are too powerful and so intricately intertwined to be coincidence. The loss of her dad at such a young age from my perspective, along with the lack of mothering her mum did, gave my mum a powerful independence that she still has. Her maturity was well beyond her years, which attests to the fact her and my dad became such a good team. He was young for his age, still very sharp and humorously quick witted which suited my mum well.

Entering primary 5 at 10 years old my anxiety came back pretty heavily. I was aware of myself, I knew that the whole world just seen me as a kid. I was learning about life more how important getting an education and being able to work with others was, learning about death for the first time and that my mum and dad wouldn't be around forever. And even I wouldn't be around forever. I don't know if this is a normal time in life to experience anxiety but when I thought of myself, self-conscious about my glasses and comparing myself to others, that sense of impending doom, that's what it was. This realisation that I was in control of who I became did two things, make me start to dream about who I was going to be and start to act as if I was that already. I remember in the hall of our house we had a big mirror on the wall that was just about neck level for me, on boring Sundays or whenever I passed it and caught my eye, I would look at myself. Not for vanity but look almost through myself and really ask myself who I was, that I was human like everyone else and that there was a me before I remember being, where did I come from? Where am I going? These questions came up for me that I'd never thought of before, this is the closest I've ever felt to a "god", this outer body experience of realising I was alive sent shivers up my spine and really took me out of my senses. Now I don't know what actually occurred if I had just got dizzy from staring through myself or if I had somehow meditated transcendently without realising but the feeling was so powerful I remember it still. I've tried a few times to replicate this but to no avail, perhaps I had less distractions then or the simple fact I had no expectations of anything coming from it and just allowed the experience. It was here I started to develop an ego, at least what the majority of the world associate "ego" with. I had felt so connected to the world it was like I was being guided and that whatever I chose to do would be great. I don't know why feeling this way sparked that confidence but as I carried it through my life from that point any deviations from my expectations were met with disgust and confusion. The vocabulary of the western world growing up seen ego as a bad thing, that being egotistical meant cocky or arrogant. Perhaps to some I was, but it never crossed my mind at the time. I felt confident in my ability to be whoever I chose to be, nothing more or less than that.

Up to this point in my education the academic side of school didn't seem to be a weak point for me until my anxiety around math and a poorly equipped teacher caused one of the few uncomfortable memories I have of primary school. This big test was coming up that would decide what level of maths and ultimately, which class we would move into. The pressure I felt to get a good mark had worried me to the point I would freeze up in class when asked a question about it. I remember being sat with the teacher at the front of the class going over my work, as she asked me how I got the answer I got so anxious I started crying as she kept asking getting more annoyed at my silence, unable to see my stress building. I didn't understand any of it and that scared me.

When my mum and dad found out about my math class incident they of course were supportive and offered to help with homework and roped my brother in to showing me how he did it. My brother has always been very smart, in school they called him Mcnoggin as our second name is McNair and he was always first in his class. For those of you not familiar to the expression "noggin" means head in Scotland. Mcnair with the big brain, became "mcnoggin". To them the fact I wasn't the best at math wasn't a shock, there are broken memories of my mum trying to teach me how to tell time as it didn't come naturally to me, numbers didn't make sense to me I needed words, I remember the same feeling as in that maths class and getting irritated when I couldn't grasp it.

My mum has said this to me many times throughout my life and reminds me still that I have always wanted to run before I could walk, I wanted to know how to do something before I had tried it. I was obsessed with cowboys as a child and even convinced my mum to get me horse riding lessons but I was annoyed I had to learn, I just wanted to jump on a horse with my lasso and take off. I had developed the love of westerns from watching them with my dad, old John Wayne movies and the magnificent seven were my favourites. This same impatience to learn came up a few times growing up, I wanted to swim but needed lessons again as it didn't come naturally. I would think of something that would take years to be the best at and expect to be that good straight away. I believe my imagination had something to do with this, I could see myself so vividly doing it and even feel myself there. With swimming I could feel the water pass through my fingers and see myself rhythmically breathing as if it was second nature to me, but the reality was weeks of flailing about in the shallow end getting water up my nose and in my eyes, with the grace and poise of an elephant getting in a bath. I think the realisation of not being as good as I thought I was, had an impact on my ego, before I knew what an ego was of course. It didn't stop me learning to swim, eventually it didn't stop me learning to ride a horse either but it put enough doubt in me to slow the jumping from one hobby to the next, as I got older. I grew to allow the imperfections in my training or new hobbies to motivate me and become more disciplined with them. Understanding that in order to really improve you have to face the obstacles just as much as the polishing of the areas you are good in. When practicing karate I would practice the moves I was bad at more than the ones I knew, this lead me to jumping through the ranks remarkably quickly. I had got a glimspe of something eternally valuable.

Outside of school I had a couple good friends to spend my evenings with, when I wasn't at football training or any of my other temporary hobbies. My best friend was liked by everyone even my mum and dad which was rare for my early companions.

He was good at football, which took away from me being average. Rangers were our team and most days after school we would play football for as long as our parents allowed. Singing songs we didn't know the history behind and talking all things football. It was like having another brother and another family when I was at his house. We were close and I still pass him in the street today and say hello. Towards the end of primary school I lost interest in pretending to like football and we started to drift apart. It didn't make me go back to football though, I had realised that I wasn't very good at it and the only thing keeping me from exploring new ventures was the social group I had gained. I think a lot of my anxiety stemmed from trying to be who I had portrayed myself as being, I had this ideal in my head to live up to and as time went on the pressure to keep it up caused me to worry about being found out as fake. I also felt as though I was lying to myself this wasn't me, what if I was wasting time I could have been spending becoming better at what I really loved I couldn't pretend anymore.

      Although I had tried many different hobbies and sports before football, having the social input changed my view of trying new things, I had done judo, karate, skateboarding, bmx, boxing, horse riding and swimming as I mentioned. Until I found rugby. I still enjoy rugby over any other sport to play the sheer brutality and physicality completely engrossed me. This was a new world to me, I could express and vent my frustations physically through the game. Agression was applauded on the field unlike in everyday life, that was huge to me. What else was possible? My brother and I both enrolled in the local team and it felt like I had found the Holy Grail. I was part of a team although a lot of them didn't go to our school, I had structure I enjoyed, I had great coaches I looked up to, and above all else I was good at it. The only issue around rugby was that my friends at school liked football and subsequently hated rugby or they egg chasers as any rugby man has heard before. This left me pretty isolated at school, all my usual friends were playing football and I no longer wanted to. I needed new friends quick to slow the anxiety that was growing the more days I found myself alone. This change came at the worst time for me as we were just about to finish school for summer be-fore going into secondary. With almost no friends and pressure to live up to my brothers academic achievements. My stress and anxiety were high, which made me irritable particularly around following routine and adults instructions. My brother and I went to a childminder now and again when my mum and dad had to work late or on school holidays or often when we weren't well and they couldn't stay at home to look after us. She was a miser-able old hag of a woman who I believe didn't actually like chil-dren and we hated being there but we knew my mum was trying to become a counsellor and my dad was working hard so we understood they had little choice. They needed us to go and be-have, so we normally played our part and behaved accordingly. But this summer we had got tired of just doing what we were told. I felt annoyed with life at this age, I was following a hobby I loved but that no one else around me at school enjoyed and I was stuck in this miserable womans house with other children of different ages all unsure why we were there. When all I wanted was to be playing ps2 at home or generally anywhere else than in her front room waiting on my mum coming to save us. One day we decided, my brother and I, to tell the childminder that we were going to a family friends house and that our mum had Ok'd it. We then talked our way past our friends mum who was actually a family friend so we didn't think it would be that bad. We played games until we guessed it was time to go home and as you can imagine we got home to a mother stressed to the point of tears as she had no idea where her two boys were for 4 hours, sorry mum.

I noticed as the summer holidays went on before second-ary that I wasn't as social as I had been in the years before, I didn't want to go play football with my old friends and no one other than my brother played rugby in our town. I felt for the first time what being bullied was, I tried to still hang about with my friends who played football but they didn't accept me as one of them anymore. I didn't get invited out anymore and on occasion they avoided me if we did bump into each other. It annoyed me more than it should have and I felt lonely and apprehensive going into first year as I thought I would end up with no friends and therefore be vulnerable to being picked on. I wouldn't be as cool as I once felt I was, there were a few sleepless nights that summer. It dawned on me though after finding my own confidence again, I wish I had a memory of how I gained my confidence back then. It wasn't there one minute and it was the next. Maybe it was engrossing myself in rugby and growing into my body more but that I decide what's cool now. I can choose to do and be whatever I want. The old friends didn't like me anyway. What did I have to lose? There was also never a physical fear for me at this age I was tall for my age and I took pride in being strong and aggressive from playing rugby, so I was confident in my ability to protect myself if someone wanted to try and bully me. I admit this thinking is simplistic juvenile male behaviour but it stopped me from worrying. I also had my big brother at the school, he was always a big guy and although he had a hard time with bullies at school himself we would have each other if things got bad. I don't know if this is a normal thought process for someone at that age but it made sense to me. My love of music had sparked a whole new side of me over summer and everyone I listened to had that cool confidence I wanted to have.So I acted as though I felt that way, when inside I was in fact quite scared.

First day of secondary school felt like a big jump in maturity, being from a small town where school was always walking distance. Getting on the bus with my big brother in the morning was freeing and scary at the same time. I was glad to have a big brother during this time. He told me where certain groups people stood in the playground and the areas for each of the different subjects were taught. He was my cheat sheet for not looking as lost as I felt. As I walk into the gates I see the group of friends I was usually with in primary but we had gone down different paths over the summer and I chose not to go stand with them. I can't remember who I spent the first few days with but was I was feeling more confident having spoken to a lot more people than I thought I would of. After a week or so two friends emerged from the mass of new faces as my new close friends, this was the weird age where we still played to an extent with bikes and ps3 and occasionally air riffles. It was also the age where we started to experiment with being adults, smoking cigarettes and stealing the odd can of beer from my dad's create in the cold store. Ultimately though my parent's voices in my head didn't allow me to indulge fully at this age.

Week days were taken up with school, homework, rugby and my newest passion the gym. I had been improving at rugby but because of my height I was playing with boys a year above me, which gave my ego a boost, to think I was tougher than I really was. Because of the age difference I was skinny for a rugby player. I probably still am to be honest. To put some weight on I followed in my brothers footsteps and went to the gym, for those of you who haven't fallen in love with training this might seem quite sad but the gym was the best thing to ever find me. I loved the feeling of the weights and the constant challenge to lift more, heavier and more reps, from here I became obsessed with watching youtube videos of old body building footage and people who would inspire me for years to come. The physical aspect of rugby and training had started to interest me more than the actual game, when I played I wanted to display my strength and fitness more than I wanted to win the match. This is why I spent most of my time learning fitness than I did learning rugby techniques. People like Greg Plitt, Christian Guzman, Matt Ogus, Steve Cook, Mike Rashid and Jeff Logan to name a few became the soundtrack to these years of my life. I was enjoying the balance I had found in life with school work, rugby, my friends and the gym. Everything had its place and almost supported each other. Things were going great for me. Until my mum and dad divorced.

I remember the feeling like it was yesterday, as if my all the small things I had chose to ignore crumbled to reveal reality. The age difference, the arguments, the lack of days out they'd had together, the increase in them going out separately. It was a sickening realisation. The thing that I knew then was why I was upset, change, in itself the changes that were going to come made me sad and angry. I didn't want change. I had found a good balance in my life with new friends and hobbies that I loved I didn't want to change that. I believe in the beginning I blamed my mum as she was the one to tell me and my brother, she was leaving my dad. She took responsibility for her part, told us it didn't mean they didn't love us anymore and that they needed to do what made them happy. I remember my mum crying and telling me she was sorry as I cried under the duvet, where I had ran when she told me. I wanted to say its okay and that I didn't blame her but I couldn't speak. The lump in my throat wouldn't let me.

I had no patience for school after this. How could learning history or maths help me fix this? I acted out pretty much straight away. No one was going to tell me what to do, adults don't know what's right either otherwise my mum and dad wouldn't have let this happen, this was my thinking. In a way it helped me find a voice of my own, before I just went along with what I was told and respected teachers and adults alike. This is how my parents raised me but now I was questioning everything. At school being more outgoing and bold was great fun, at that age anything from the norm is attractive and being a bit rebellious is still cool. I spoke back to teachers to be funny in class. I wouldn't bring a bag as I thought it made me cooler but it caused more trouble than it was worth. When I had forgotten my homework that I had normally still had done. I had a few girlfriends during this time but nothing serious, it wasn't that I wasn't interested I just didn't see the point it wasn't like we were going to be together forever. I'm aware this outlook may have come from the divorce, knowing that even when you think it's "happily ever after" nothing lasts forever. The more I thought of this the more independent I felt, why would I listen to teachers? They had went from school, to college, to university and back to school. No part of their life interested me or made me want to listen and take their advice. I was naive to education I believed if I was good enough and smart enough that the degree or bit of paper with a qualification on it wouldn't matter. I was wrong, to an extent but I still feel strongly about this, that someone who can do the job well and passionately should get the job over someone just because they went to university for example. Add to this I was constantly watching young entrepreneurs doing what I wanted to do, making it look easy. I had this over powering feeling that I would make it someday, that I would be someone I was proud to be. I had to grow up fast though I told myself, I can't waste any more time listening to these people who have nothing I wanted, it seemed to me at the time anyway. With this new claimed independence came a real fear of responsibility, my future was no longer mapped out in front of me by my parents. I felt lied to, mislead, the more I learned of other people's success.It was made clear by my parents that to be successful in life school was crucially important, and although they may have been pushing for me to get an education and actually learn something I took it literally, as in the work the teachers were giving me was in itself important to know. Leaving me of course sceptical very quickly when sitting in maths learning about triangles and in french trying to translate as best I could from looking at the pictures. How was this going to make me better than someone without an education? I still have never used anything from those classes and hope I never have to. I was missing the point of course but at the time with my teenage blinkers on the future and adulthood I couldn't help but feel like it was a waste of time. Often the people I was looking up to online were not doctors or academics, but high achievers and hard workers in their field, they had the money cars and houses that I wanted But more than that they seemed to have freedom in their lives they weren't working 9-5 monday to friday and listening to a boring grey faced teacher all day, that was enough for me to trust their input more than the adults in front of me.

   The first weekend after my mum told me she was leaving my dad I decided I was going to have a drink. I'm still 13 at this point and although the odd beer or glass of wine was allowed on special occasions to try, I had never been drunk or even tipsy before. My close friends were up for it as well either due to their own interest or not wanting to be left out. We had realised the mutual friends I used to have before secondary started were no different from us now. Football wasn't played as much and didn't matter anymore. We had all reached out to curb the awkwardness of being the new kids at the school and we ended up as a pretty big group. That weekend we had saved our lunch money, asked the local alcoholic to jump in the shop for us and got drunk. I don't remember much from this night but at some point I'd not text my mum back enough times that she had come out and found me, drunk and presumably not fit to look after myself. She was surprisingly calm, not as angry with me as I had thought, perhaps understanding that I was testing her authority and being rebellious as most teenagers are. She did however explain to me that drinking on the street was something "wee bams" did and that I could have a drink when I was older and under her supervision. She didn't say it in these terms but she didn't want me to become part of that group. I didn't see it as she did however, to me they were just my friends and we were all experimenting together with adulthood or what we thought being an adult was at the time. If you grew up in Scotland you'll understand the term young team, if not I'll try and explain the absurdity as well as I can, even though we were a small town so small that we needed three towns to fill the school, which wasn't that big, we would fight with our peers from different towns. To either pass the time or because of some mythical made up reason that made it seem cooler than it was. Naturally having gave all adults and authority the finger in my life at this point I seen it as a good excuse to gain some popularity and vent some frustrations. I'm not going to go into the fights I was involved in and who with because it's embarrassing to even remember it. However it didn't go unnoticed by the school or my parents, unfortunately.

My Mum had moved out at this point with my big brother and I chose to stay with my dad, due to a number of reasons. I felt my mum had just got bored of being different ages with him and their lifestyles drifted from what they wanted out of life, although I kept thinking my mum should have thought of that when she started the relationship. My dad was also showing his age more at this point he was about 63-64 and I was now taller and stronger than him I felt he somehow needed protected, not that he needed it in fact during the fighting and rebellious time of my youth he threw a boy over our garden fence who was chasing me after an earlier scuffle. I also chose to stay with my dad because on the night of my mum leaving. I was going to bed and passed his room to say goodnight, like I always did, I found him crying, with a look on his face and demeanour that will stay with me till I die. He looked defeated, like his heart was breaking in front of me. For the first time I seen him as a human with flaws and emotions instead of this all powerful cool all the time character he was through my rose tinted glasses. I just gave him a hug and said I wasn't going anywhere, no matter what. See my dad had a family before he met my mum. A wife two boys and a daughter. We never met them as all connections had been frayed to a point of separation by the time I was born. He had had an affair with my mum but gave his ex-wife all he owned. The house, the car, financial support for the children and even his dog, a dog he had trained from a puppy himself long before he ever met his wife to be, and not just trained to the point it didn't chew the couch. But to the point he could walk with him off the lead, tell him to stay then cross the road go into the post office then the butchers or whatever else he had to do before meeting the golden retriver who would still be patiently waiting in the exact same spot. My point with that is he put the time in, he went to a great deal of effort to invest his time and energy into something for her just to take it due to lawyers and paperwork, a brutal life loop hole I deeply disagree with.I knew he followed his heart to be with my mum and had done his best to support and be in his children's lives. Only for them to turn their backs on him. There was no way I was leaving him too. He didn't say anything through his tears but his hand just patted the back of my head letting me know he'd heard me. That night I didn't sleep, I was up daydreaming of how I could change this for him, how I could make enough money so he wouldn't stress as much. How could I support myself so he didn't have to worry as much as he did? I helped as much as I could around the house after that. We had decided to stay where we lived until I finished school it made sense, for the moment but it was strange living in that house without my brother and my mum.

My mum only entered that house once more while my dad was still there. I forget everything previously until this day, I walked past our dog teddy in the hall that afternoon, and she looked as she always did peaceful content and sleeping. I lay down next to her as I had since I was a child, it wasn't until I put my face up to hers and looked at her now cataract eyes that I noticed something wasn't right. She would often move her head away so as to not be so close but she never moved. I sat up and saw she was breathing very shallow and sharply, I called my dad from his living room and he had a look at her. As he tried to get her to stand it was clear she wasn't right. We phoned the vet straight away and they explained her stomach may have twisted as it was common in her breed. We had to get her to the vet, a 30 minute drive away. I remember getting her towel we used especially for her and having to carry her to the car. She lay with her head in my lap the whole journey clearly becoming restless as she realised in herself something was wrong. I knew she was older and that if it was anything serious she might not make it, thirteen years' worth of memories flashed through me on that half hour drive. The time she jumped through the window at an old castle we visited and we thought she was gone forever, just for her to run round the corner as if it was the most fun she'd ever had. Or the time I walked past her in the hall and she was chewing a huge ball of hubba-bubba bubble gum, she had found in the bin in my room. The way she would come sit between my legs on the couch and have me play with the ungrown-into puppy fat on her neck. When she knocked my mum down the kitchen steps in her excitement to see her and broke my mums' ankle. The time she went on a journey herself after finding a hole in the fence only to be brought back by the old woman down the road who had found her in her bed. She was everything you wanted from a pet and the scale of the potential loss we faced as a family grew as we drove. It didn't take long for the vet to confirm our fears, her stomach had twisted and she needed surgery, but they didn't think she would be strong enough to survive it. Ultimately it was up to me and my dad to put her down there an then and not make her suffer or go through the extensive,painful,unpromised, recovery. I was uncontrollably crying as they explained what was going to happen, just a small jag in her leg and she would go to sleep. I knew it was the right thing to do so I never questioned it I just looked into her eyes the whole time softly saying thank you and that I loved her as she passed away. I had phoned my mum to tell her we were on the way to the vet and the situation but I could no longer speak to tell her she'd gone. We decided to take her home an bury her out the back garden, that we'd built as a family, it seemed only right for her to stay at home, where she'd always been. As we got home my brother had came to help bury her and say goodbye and my mum was on her way from work. My brother tried to comfort me but I felt selfish taking any comfort she was our dog not just mine and I wanted to do right by her. My dad got the shovels out the shed and handed me one, I started digging but as the thoughts in my head grew my anger at the situation and and frustrations of not being able to change it caused me to break the shovel in half. This was a heavy duty workmans shovel too not a lightweight wooden one, the adrenaline and emotion had gave me strength I didn't know I had. Along with the recent changes in our family living dynamic with my mum moving out it was too much for me to process, My dad opened a cider and have me a glass, told me it was okay and calmed me down a bit. My tears stopped as we finished and moved her body from her bed wrapped in her favourite blankets with her toy. When my mum arrived I felt the loss all over again seeing her reaction. We said our goodbyes and as time passed I came to terms with what had happened, as I reminded myself she had had a great life with a family who loved her dearly. The house seemed quieter than ever now with just me and my dad in this big house. I had more time with my thoughts in the coming weeks and my resentment of the reality in front of me grew.

  This caused a divide between me and my family for a bit, I gave my mum attitude when I was with her as the thought of my dad crying that night stayed with me and played on my mind. This led me to only visit my mum a couple times a week despite staying in the same town. My mum was stricter than my dad, she was now a qualified counsellor and dealing with horror stories and people who had experienced the worst life has to offer on a daily basis. This made her short tempered with my "nothing can touch me" attitude. I didn't stop going out either, My dad was easier to convince as long as I came home at a reasonable time and didn't look completely steaming he let a lot slide. He had made it very clear that if I had ever got so drunk beyond the point of being able to protecting myself that he would break my legs. A rule that had been given to him by his dad. After waking up one morning to his dad seething at the kitchen table, his dad simply said "have you seen your brother" and pointed to the room. My dad entered to find his older brother on a blood soaked pillow with his face cut all over. He had been glassed in a pub and been too drunk to protect himself. My dad vouched to never drink to that point and had passed that on to me. I wasn't drinking a lot in my eyes it was just a few beers on the weekend after rugby with my friends, but an itch to experiment further was creeping into our conversations.

At school there had been a couple of incidents with boys from the other town that had caused me to be under the campus policeman's radar, they brought my mum and dad in after the second fight, in as many weeks, to sit down and talk to me. They sat in a circle with the head of my year and the deputy head teacher my mum, dad and the policeman. I had no interest in listening to them, I didn't feel they would listen to me anyway. Not all the fights were my fault I did get harassed a few times where I felt I had no choice. They also weren't particularly violent incidents just usual school boy scuffles. I refused to be honest with them and tell them that I didn't want to come to school and have to avoid these people I kept clashing with, I didn't want to seem as though I was being bullied or that I couldn't handle it myself. I wanted the respect they had, to be spoke to as equal and until then I wasn't saying anything. I did get emotional after this sit down. I realised perhaps I was on the wrong path despite feeling as though I was trying to do well. I was overwhelmed by the feeling of isolation, they didn't listen to me they had already labelled me a "ned"- a non-educated delinquent- translation if you're not native to Scotland. I couldn't lie to myself I wanted to be aggressive, I was angry after losing our dog and my family dynamic. The family outside of us was already gone, in my mind they weren't really family just relations and I never thought that would happen between my mum, dad,brother and me. It felt as though I was stuck in the middle. Until I was old enough to look after myself.

To help keep me from causing more trouble for myself I decided to focus on rugby, I joined the school team and upped the training in the gym with my brother. I almost immediately felt better, my confidence grew from training with someone older than me and pushing myself physically. Our rugby team was doing well too, we won the league that year and I was scouted for the district team try outs. I was feeling in control again, if I focused on what made me feel good, training and rugby. Then the negative feelings from school and family didn't seem so bad.

I had received a punching bag for my 14th birthday which was a heavy duty UFC standard bag with the full bracket that was screwed into the wall with six, six inch bolts. I loved this bag, I would do rounds in the house and then run up and down the stairs to maintain my cardio in the winter for rugby. I also started to develop a useful skill where I would channel the frustrations and anger from, my mum leaving, my dog dying, the pressure from school, the pressure I put on myself to be good at everything I tried to do. I used it in my training to push me further. With only training techniques learned from youtube I got particularly focused one day and managed to punch this bag completely out the wall. The bracket came down on top of my dad who was holding the bag for me. I was shocked. *I was able to do this!*, although there may have been an issue with the bracket, I'm not considering myself superhuman. Once I knew my dad was alright, I was left with a great feeling of confidence in myself. I noticed it had been the emotions I was feeling that caused the sudden increase in power. I had an epiphany that if I could use my emotions to do this then what else was I capable of it was a goose bump evoking feeling. Not only would this give me a different level of motivation it would give me a productive outlet for the emotions and the often confusing feelings I had when facing them.

Other than my birthday at 14 I didn't have a drink either. I had found a girlfriend to spend time with, who in all honesty, I was only interested in because I lost my virginity with her and that made me feel more like an adult. I notice in hind sight that I was almost narcissistic in my early relationships, it was all about how it made me look and feel instead of building a genuine connection. I am only 16 here so please don't judge.

I had had some success with rugby before, touring Ireland with our team and winning leagues but the district team was a big step up for me, if I wanted to be professional this was the path I had to be on. I played as best I could but I didn't get through. I wish I had taken my time and tried again the following year but in my haste to achieve, if I wasn't going to be the best at something I didn't want to do it. It goes back to me wanting to run before I could crawl again but at the time I didn't realise this and my love for rugby faded over the next few months. I felt like what's the point? In training for something I wasn't going to do forever. My motivation to train even in the gym decreased as I had no aim for my sessions anymore. I fell into a bad habit with my eating as my mum wasn't at home cooking and as much as my dad tried he wasn't as good as my mum. Everyone's mum is the best cook to them but I'm actually right, there wasn't a meal I remember not enjoying that she cooked for us, I would watch her prepare everything from scratch all fresh healthy ingredients and create something amazing from it.

I chose to go out again at weekends as I didn't have rugby keeping me occupied, I experimented with weed as my love for music grew. All the artists I looked up to talked about smoking and my curiosity lead me to trying it myself. I don't remember the feeling it was just something to do with my friends, naively the friends I was doing it with didn't have any ambition and were doing it for the feeling and to get a buzz while I was mostly pretending I was a musician and a creative type. I also drank every weekend almost without fail I would drink at least one day at the weekend to the point I was drunk. We didn't cause any trouble though we were just bored stuck in a small town surrounded with nothing but fields and trees, I'm not making excuses, there were of course more productive things I could have been doing but after rugby not going to plan and having no plans for my future, other than get rich quick,I enjoyed the numbing effect it had on my emotions. If I was spending time with my friends drunk and doing nothing at least I wasn't aware of the responsibility I was ignoring, the pressure I had gave myself to support my dad and live up to the man I wanted to be.

At home I started to enjoyed the freedom in the house with it just being my dad and I, I didn't have to fight with my brother for the PlayStation or the tv remote. We had two living rooms in the house so when I had friends round we had space to ourselves. Just to play PlayStation games and talk about girls mostly. Academically this was an important year for me as I'd sit my exams at the end of it, despite my best efforts I struggled to find motivation in class, I would always get to the end of the lesson an realise I hadn't done a lot and tell myself I'll do more tomorrow. The only class I was doing well in was English, I enjoyed the imaginative writing. Having developed a vast imagination as child playing by myself, words allowed me to paint the picture in my head on to paper. I went on to get very mediocre exam results as I didn't study seriously as I felt that if I at least didn't try hard I wouldn't feel bad about failing. Although I paid the results no mind, I found out the following year that my assessment piece of writing was being used to teach the following students. I had a great deal of pride when I found out. It supported my belief, if you're good enough you don't need that piece of paper, a degree, it shouldn't hold you back. I had no desire to go on and do Highers or go to university either .I wanted to start making money as soon as possible. I think this desire to make money straight away came from watching my parents, together they were comfortable but apart I watched my dad stress about money and seen my mum go from this big house we shared to a smaller less attractive council house. I wanted to shock them from my rebellious nature at school that I could still provide and make a good living on my own.

At 15 after my exams I left school, I didn't have a master plan but I knew I had to make money and the quickest way to do this was working with my dad. Although being a dental technician required going to college I had spent a summer working there to keep me out of trouble and I had grasped it enough for the owners of the lab to let me work. I was only just about to turn 16 so they didnt have to pay me a lot and the vouch from my dad was enough for them to higher me full time. The hours were half 7-4 Monday to Thursday and an early finish on the Friday. I spent the morning casting impressions, to create a plaster model of the patients' teeth. You see the dentist decides what needs done and what crowns and veneers the patient needs but they then send that to us for the manufacturing bit. Once the impressions had been cast I spent the afternoon casting dentures, pressing acrylic into the moulds through a process that took skill and practice to perfect. I enjoyed it for the first few months feeling more like an adult and getting better at the job itself. The reality of money and income started to wear me down the more I gained knowledge on living costs and the price of my favourite things. I started to pay rent to my dad as soon as I started work.I appreciate this from him now but at the time I was heartbroken he was taking my hard earned cash from me.It taught me early on that you need to be responsible with your money and that things that have greater value financially are attainable but require you to do make the money first. I was getting over minimum wage for my age but for what I wanted to do with it, it wasn't enough to invest wisely in big things like a house or business of my own. But also not light enough to stop me from enjoying it foolishly. As I'm sure we all did at some point I spent my money on clothes and things I would later rarely if ever use again. The voice in my head repeating "I deserve it" and "what am I working for if I can't enjoy it?" caused some valuable lessons for me. I was getting to the end of the month with little to no savings I was discouraged from any dream I thought of becoming with this outlook, where I was too far away from where I was trying to be. I put my dreams to the back of my mind and took it a week at a time. Enjoying the money when I could, on more materialistic clothing or fancy bottle of alcohol to feel as though I had more than I did.

My trajectory in work had slowed down, the next steps in dental techitionary were hard to teach while running a business and the time spent on my development was menial each week. Add to this there was a man in the work who decided since I was the youngest and an easy target that he would periodically try to bully and belittle me day in and day out. Nothing so severe it was worth reporting, not that I ever would, but just poking at me. Calling me wee man and genuinely being a bit of a dick. I managed to be the bigger man for the majority of the time but making sure it didn't go too far where he thought he could continue with the daily barrage of poor taste colloquialism.

It was a few months into my new job when my dad and I decided to move out from rattling around the big house and move from the small town back to where my dad felt at home, Glasgow. I had mixed emotions of this at the time, the circumstances had occurred to where my mum actually made an offer to my dad to buy him out. So the family home was still in the family, I was just not going to be there with my dad anymore. My mum had met a new man by this point as well, someone more her age and definitely her type with the same masculine energy as my dad, if not more. He seemed like a decent guy but I paid him no attention for a long time, I was 16 he wasn't there to be my step father as long as he made my mum happy it didn't bother me. My dad I later found out had a thing with a woman for a while but not serious enough to tell me or my brother. He had decided to spend more time enjoying life, he had worked for over 40 years at this point and could retire in the next 5 years if he chose to not that he had any plans.

During the transitional period when it was planned we were going to sell and move, I chose to make the most of being able to see my friends as much as I could. I got into a bit of a habit that even thinking about today makes me feel sick to my stomach. I wasn't training, I was smoking cigarettes my diet was terrible, my teenage heart had been broken by a girl for the first time, by my childhood sweetheart and I felt almost numb to my own existence. A humbling experience for the same young man who used to meditate transcendently by merely looking at himself in a mirror. I would work at the lab as usual but by Thursday night I was already planning my weekend inebriation while smoking the first few joints of the week. Friday night ment a crate of beer often bought by my dad as he was told it would last me the week and I would only have a few each night, although I always got more. On Friday depending on how my week had went I would go to a friend's house or wherever we were all meeting and drink and make plans for the following day. My dad understood I wanted to make the most of seeing my friends before we moved and allowed me to have friends over for parties as the house was big enough that we wouldn't disrupt him reading the paper in the next room. It became a known thing that my house was good for parties which lead to me feeling part of a big group of friends when in reality I think a lot of people used me to facilitate their own teenage experiences.

Girls were not hard for me to pull either with it being my house they would flirt with me to get in then my natural way of being with the "don't give a fuck attitude" lent itself to very fond and egotistically driven nights and experiences that I won't divulge. I felt good having people around me and being in the spotlight occasionally from having the parties, albeit the genuine friendships it created were almost non-existent.

It was also on a Friday where we bought our drugs for the weekend. By the time I was 16 I was taking cocaine every week, it had only been once or twice before this that I had tried it. Granted it was not loads and it wasn't as pure as it is today, and whatever other excuse you may believe. On occasion I also bought ecstasy although only a couple of times on a rare Saturday with decent plans. Sunday I would either be still drunk or in a friend's house most of the day before coming home at dinner time to sleep before work, or be able to walk earlier and spend the day smoking weed and talking about the night before. I had no direction, I was hurting in ways I didn't understand until later and it just seemed normal after a while.

My curiosity behind taking the drugs and alcohol was always something I heard in music or through the guys at my work, I didn't think the danger was real I thought like everything, bored scared adults had make them seem worse than it was and the creative and cool types from my eyes took them like it was a part of daily life. The guys at my work were always talking about how fucked up they had been at my age and how they still took them. They seemed to have money as well or at least not the down an out homeless type of addict you hear more about. They wore designer clothes and had tattoos and had a reputable job, they couldn't be that bad.

My whole binge lifestyle only peaked to this extent for around four months, I became aware of the damage I was doing to myself eventually. One night where I'd taken ecstasy for the first time my friend was stabbed in an altercation not far from where we had been drinking, the crash from hearing the news while on the top of an mdma high made me never want to do it again. The depth of depression I felt the following days felt like it would never leave me, I eventually had to take another half a pill to get me out of the downward spiral. With cocaine it was after a night where I let my ego get the better of me, I was sitting with a group that was older than me and to prove I fitted in I bought too much for me to handle. Although I always shared I must have taken more than enough to kill a 17 year old which I was , what insued the following day is the least connected to the world I have ever felt. It was like I was someone else for the day, my whole demeanour changed I felt stupid my thoughts were making no sense to me and I was genuinely frightened I'd caused irreversible damage. Add to that the bill I woke up to was more than what I now pay for rent. Add to this feeling the morning nosebleeds and heart palpitations that lasted into the following days my experimentation with coke had reached its crescendo. To try and feel normal again I didn't drink or take anything the following few days then when I felt somewhere close to normal I went out for a "social" drink and smoke with my friends. I remember it had been a bottle of really nice vodka brought back from my dad's travels I had asked him to pick up for me. We were drinking it with redbull and playing a smoking game where you see who can hold the smoke in for the longest time. Now looking back I can see the stupidity of mixing weed with redbull itself not to mention the vodka as well. It wasn't long before I started feeling pains in my chest and light headed, the paranoia grew enough for me to make up an excuse and leave for home. It took hours for the anxiety to pass having to explain to my dad what I had been doing as I genuinely felt close to death. I vowed to myself that I would add weed to the list of things I wasn't doing again.

My view of the town I found myself in began to change as I looked at it in a sober mind, just because there was a group of us drinking like this didn't mean it was normal. It wasn't leading anywhere positive and you could see it in the faces of the older boys, I remember a conversation with one of them where I was explaining my bad drug experiences as he was taking ecstasy. He turned and said "once you realise life is going to be shit, you stop caring and trying to be anything else" as he swallowed the pill. I was disgusted in myself that I'd let myself fall into a group who's mindset was that. I did feel lost and often depressed but I always had this hope inside me trusting that it would get better and things would change. I think looking back I always justified my actions and ignored the reality of what I was doing, I was in pain but It was made worse by using it as an excuse rather than allowing myself to feel it and move past it. I remember this day vividly it was the middle of the day on a sunday and I was drunk already, not knowing how to face the damage I had caused to my life. I knew that no more alcohol or drug would make me feel what I was searching for I had to choose a different path. The group I was with decided to go to a friends house and asked me to come. In that moment I knew I had to walk away, I said I was going home and I never drank with them again. I was moving to glasgow in the following week and the fear of leaving my home town and friends left me and was replaced with the peace of having a fresh start. I could be anyone I wanted to be in Glasgow, no one knew me, I still had a job, I could get back into a positive routine and find my way back to the path of my earlier dreams. Although the road infront of me looked daunting I knew the alternative was where I was and anywhere looked better than this.

As me and my dad settled into our new flat I came to terms with the change in space, we were now in a two bedroom flat in a busy part of the city. A big change from the rural settings and big house we were used to. It was however a lovely area as my dad knew Glasgow well and wouldn't live anywhere else. With some form of saving grace my brother had acquired some gym equipment and weights throughout the years that I had convinced him to sell me. Along with the punching bag I already had I set up a home gym in my room. I felt if I was to spend money on a gym membership I may aswell get back to a decent fitness level myself first. I completely engulfed myself in fitness and health, any spare moment I was on youtube watching my idols who had improved again from my break in training. The motivation and teachings from youtube alone was enough for me to change my body and mindset. I learned about the science behind building muscle and gaining weight and knew that with discipline I could continue to improve. I had no distractions either, throught the week I would work and train. My friends were all 45 minutes away in the town I grew up in. I had found a path atleast for my health, I knew if I was healthy and looked after myself I would become stronger and things would be easier to face and hopefully work out. My determination in hinesight came from trying to make up for how reckless I'd been with my health, as if trying to erase the damage in a panic. Although a great way to stay commited I feel I replaced the addiction of feeling numb with drugs and alcohol, with being robotic and unforgiving with myself. When I didn't train enough or ate poorly I would tear myself down mentally, I would tell myself I had to be better. Looking back I see it was necessary for me to be so harsh with myself but it wasn't a healthy outlook on health and fitness. As I would unfortunately learn the hard way.

I still visited my mum and seen some friends now an then, but I had chose to attach myself to the older, quieter group that I knew and despite a few nights socially drinking in their house there was no desire to take anything else or drink too much. I had found a balance where I worked hard through the week and every other weekend I would have a drink and visit my friends. Things between me and my mum were still highly strung when I would visit it wouldn't take much for us to argue about what I was going to do with my future. They felt like the same conversations she had with me when I was drinking a lot and I felt she only seen me being a bit of a tear away. Dispite me knowing the changes I had made it irritated me that she perhaps didn't see them straight away. She was still my mum though and whatever relationship we had I knew would get better with time as she seen me make positive changes. I had began a somewhat serious relationship with a girl from the town aswell which ment I had other reasons to visit. The more time I spent at my mums the better our relationship got. We caught up with each other about what had really happened between her and my dad. It was the first time she felt I listened to her side of the story, I understood more and found peace with the fact it had worked out better for her, and even my dad was now enjoying being in glasgow and seeing his friends more. The counselling side of my mum started to intregue me, I had experienced first hand a considerable change in my mental state and wanted to have the volcabulary to understand it better, what actually happened. Without indulging her with all the details I explained why I rebelled and felt lost. Her calming nature and understanding of these feelings lifted a weight off my shoulders. She explained I would of probably have always rebelled at that age and that with the hightened emotional state from the break up had perhaps made it more extreme than it should have been. It opened up a stream of consistent communication between us for the first time in a few years. She guided me through some of the big emotional changes in my life from that point.From the anxiety I felt when being back in the town ,as it made me think of the things I had done and who I was at that time,to my relationship with the girl I was with and the reality of a loving relationship, as all my experience in this department was shallow uncaring relationships with girls I didn't even try to get to know better.Even the bullying from the guy at work, who she had worked with before and wasn't surprised we were clashing. For the first time I had an internal dialogue with my emotions, I no longer avoided them deliberately I felt I grew a lot as an individual during this period.

I started to find more depth in my relationships with friends. The conversations changed from small insignificant things to dreams and outlooks on life, what we wanted to do and what mattered to us. I started to see a more positive future, where I had friends who supported me and realising that maybe we would be in this experience together instead of feeling like I had to have all the answers. Close friends had cried on my shoulder over a number of different things. Things I was in no way qualified to handle, these issues left me thinking what could I of said there to help or ease their pain even slightly, it became an obsession. I did feel good being there for them,although not to the level I had hoped to be, just doing my best to empathise and comfort them. The ability to empathise had always been natural for me, I think I got it from my mum, but even when I was very young.My mum tells me of a time where I toddled into a room where she had been counselling, not formally, my dads neice who was going through a messy divorce and depression. They stopped talking as I entered the room but I could sense something was up and without them saying anything I just looked up and my cousin and asked "what's up?". With the age difference of my dad she was my cousin but she was in her mid thirties and I was only 3 or 4 at the time. My cousin had a shocked look on her face as I said this and looked at my mum, my mum explained that nothing was wrong that they were talking grown up stuff an that I was to leave. I didn't understand why she had said nothing was wrong I believed myself that something was wrong but at that age I just let it go an toddled out of the room looking for my big brother. Of course having this depth of empathy and loyalty to my friends would teach me another painful lesson in life.

I had a really close friend between all the different groups of friends I just associated with. Someone who had been there for a few years now and we had fond memories together, he was like a brother to me.I knew his family well and they treated me as such. We had done the usual thing teenagers do and plan a future where we were still friends for years and had built a genuine friendship for a number of years, I felt nothing could get between us we had never argued before. One night in a drunken disagreement we had came to blows in the street and I had burst his lip. In my shock of what I'd just done the first thing I thought of was to do try an explain this to his family. I thought they would understand and talk to both of us after we sobered up. I hoped it would just be a speedbump in our friendship and that we would get over it. But as I'm walking towards his house with him.We were still arguing with each other but I felt we both thought it would get resolved as quickly as it happened.He then changed his voice and started sounding really hurt, I turned to see he was on the phone and as I turned back around I could see figures running towards me through the dark. We had only been a few hundred yards from his house, he had phoned his dad who was in the house with cousins of my once friend, he had played it to them as if I had just attacked him. His dad and two other guys I recognised as his cousins came out the dark infront of me. I tried to explain and put my hands up defensively but his dad didn't even change his speed towards me and started swinging punches at me. My heart sank I couldn't believe he had turned on me that quick with no chance of hearing me out.Five years I had been his close friend and had never done anything to mistreat him or his family but this is how they treated me after all my loyalty. It wasn't just that night either he had older cousins who wanted their pound of flesh from me for protecting myself. I never trusted another friend fully after this it also made it easier to leave the town when we moved.

The lesson stays with me though.

The change in lifestyle gave me more money as I wasn't spending it all on drungs and alcohol, I paid my dad digs which felt good, I had finally reached a point I could offer some support. My new found vessel for my money came in the form of tattoos. Like everything I grew to enjoy I had seen them in movies and in music videos I watched on youtube.Again the successful creative types I aspired to be like had them, not all of them granteed but I loved anything artistic and that set me out as different from who I was surrounded by. I dont know where this feeling came from, it wasn't who I was surrounded by but what they represented to me the same mistakes I'd made around drugs and alcohol. I regret my first tattoo now but at the time it was my pride and joy, I was acting and trying to reinvent myself as more than I was. I went through a phase of getting them every month and had almost finished a sleeve before things changed.I also went on a couple of lads holidays with my older friends, I was only 17 on the first one but I looked as old as the friends I was with and the laws in these areas are not as strict as the uk. They were weeks filled with everything I had hoped for the sense of freedom and adulthood. The friends I went with were sensible aswell, no drugs. I was happy with myself for being able to control myself when it came to them, I had no desire to experiment as I already knew what the led to.Alcoholism runs on both sides of my family and I had scared myself with how far I could take it before I stopped. My dads brother had been an alcoholic for years and it played on my mind often, was it in my nature or genetics to fall into his footsteps? I had to be conscious of my addictions constantly as I knew to well the feeling of the world sliding under my feet as the alcohol took leverage on my behaviour. My friends started to argue near the end of our second holiday and I felt there wouldn't be a third, I was right but I had experienced it and could tick it off the list.

At home I had started to enjoy visiting my mums again, she had bought her second dog just before moving back into our family home. I always enjoyed seeing them and catching up with my mum was like therapy for me, I could ask her questions around why I was feeling or thinking a certain way and she would talk it through with me. I also still had the girlfriend in the town and we were getting to that age her mum and dad let me stay over when I was there. She had been in our social group for a while but if anything she was more of a friend than a girlfriend never the less I enjoyed the ease of the relationship so continued it with her. I also worked and lived 40 minutes away most of the week so I didn't see her all the time, which I still think is healthy for a relationship especially at that age. Allowing yourself space to grow your own outllooks and beliefs around love and relationships without the constant mirror of the other person persuading you otherwise. It was something I don't feel she did though after a while. I felt pressure to be attentive and affectionate when it didn't come naturally to me.As though I had to convince her everytime I was with her that I was interested. I appreciate this is also insecurities from her part as I have been in the same position before but at the time I didn't realise that's what it was. She was someone to talk to through the week at work it broke up the routine but I didn't love her.

Work had started to get the better of me the guy who used to wind me up was getting more consistent. My strength training had made me bigger than him now and my patience for his remarks were wearing thin. One day on our lunch break he was doing all he could to annoy me, taking his time with the microwave even though he could see I was waiting for it. I never said anything as I knew he would just take even more time if he knew it was bothering me. After another 10 minutes of him looking smug with himself he noticed I was becoming angry, he knew he had been winding me up a lot but he never changed. He said "do you want to hit me or something?" I jokingly said "nah your sitting down, that would be wrong". Something my dad had taught me, never kick a man when hes down, I of course in my adolescence taking it literally. My dad was also off that day so the guy was making the most of him not being there by annoying me with no let up. The guy returned my comment with "you wouldn't hit me anyway wee man". This pushed me over the edge, I'd worked hard to be the size I was and make the grown up decisions in life to change from where I was and I felt he had belittled that. He also felt like authority to me which I had always struggled with, that condescending feeling that loomed over my school years came back to me in that moment. All the frustrations of being in that job with no clear path forward and no one seeing me for who I was trying to become. I had been patient with this guy before, told him when he was going too far and tried to find another way to deal with him but this was the last straw. I told him to stand up then if he didn't think I would hit him, without hesitation he stood up and turned to me with that smug look on his face. I knew he wasn't a push over from spending time with him and his big brother also worked in the same building and I was nervous as to what was going to happen, I knew I couldn't just hit him once as that might give him time to retaliate before people would break it up and I was still only 16 and almost 15 years younger than he was. I punched him with eveything I had right in the face. Either the force of the punch or the surprise that I had actually hit him caused him to spin round with shouts from the other workers deafening any thoughts I had, I punched him another few times before someone broke it up. From me hitting him to being driven home by the boss was only the space of 5 minutes. The awkwardness of getting my stuff and ignoring the threats from the guy and his brother as his eye swelled up, was eerily quiet in my head. I didn't care about what they were saying I wasn't scared of them physically, I was worried about what my dad would say. I was worried they would press charges and that I could be in serious trouble. My dad was disappointed but not surprised, he told me he had said to the owners before about that guy bullying people and that it was only a matter of time before someone stood up to him. The work got in touch the next day and said that if I took unemployment they wouldn't press charges so I now had no job. I felt cheated, I had done everything I could to stop him harrassing me. I had stood up to a bully which my dad had always supported I should, it also felt right to me that he shouldn't be allowed to walk over me the way he did but none of that mattered. I was the one who suffered from it, I now had no job and was in a worse situation than he was because of my actions.

This was a hard pill to swallow after having changed my mindset drastically in a positive way, I feared I had slipped back to my ignorant ways. I went to my mum about this feeling shift and she spoke with me about my issue with authority and where it came from. I confessed I didn't know what to do with my life and she told me it was entirely up to me, that I could be anything I wanted to be if I wanted it enough. She told me to *just do something* as if that in itself would help me find my way better than just sitting waiting for inspiration. The next week or so I must have thought of thousands of things I "could" do but there was no calling to anything specific. After speaking with my dad who was often more blunt than my mum he said similarly that I could do anything I put my mind to but that I had to do something. His motivation for saying so perhaps slightly heavier than that of my mums, as he wasn't paying for the both of us when I was able to work. He also made me go to the job centre for my job seekers allowance, at least then I would have some money coming in. Although the thought of entering that pace filled me with dread I knew I had to try an fix my mistake. At the time job seekers allowance was £60 per week. It hit me just how reckless I had been with my money when I worked at the lab. From more than £65 a day to less than that a week felt like the ground had been pulled out from under my feet.

I spend about a week looking into different courses and apprenticeships but again nothing jumped out at me. They all reminded me of defeat, this wasn't who I was supposed to be just another cog in the machine like everyone else. I believed I was different although the reality showed me perhaps I wasn't. I would still continueously watch videos on youtube with these fitness entreprenuers and think anything less than that wasn't worth doing or being. They stood for something, worked for themselves, carved a way through the everyday struggles and the weight of societal pressures to be something more. I knew that a few of them had started their companies after leaving the army and that planted a seed for me. What if I went to the army, they would give me the discipline I needed to be like these people. I could work up and be a PT in the army and travel over the world with them leading training exercises. This ticked every box I had been thinking of, I had no close friends in Glasgow at the time and the friends in my town were barely close anymore either they wouldn't miss me. I could support my dad, I could send him money as I wouldn't be spending it during training. I was qualified enough, what else am I good for I thought why not risk everything for something apparently better.

It takes a long time to go through the process of joining the army. A lot longer than I wanted it to be, as time went on it was becoming harder to reinforce this plan to my parents. They knew better than me that I wouldn't like being told what to do all the time and not being able to see them. I shrugged it off thinking maybe that's exactly what I need, because I don't listen to what I tell myself to do either. Although being completely without work for the few months leading up to leaving for the army ,I had found, for the first time since finding rugby, a purpose to be better. My training sky rocketted, I would live almost the exact same day, over and over again. I was eating to gain weight training in the morning and running at night. I was reading about mindsets and people who had overcome adversities to reach great success from first controlling and understanding their minds. I was obsessed with learning how to be better, I wanted basic training to feel like a warm up to me I focused on improvement day in and day out. In my reasearch I read for the first time about the law of attraction from the book "The Secret", this became my go to tool whenever I wanted to stop or doubted myself. I envisioned who I wanted to be and worked towards it. I wrote affirmations before I went to sleep and meditated as much as I could and I seen first hand how it started to build me back up mentally and physically. I wanted to prove everyone wrong, the teachers the fake friends and the voice in my head that once led me to being a waste of space teenager. I put real distance between who I was before now that wasn't me anymore.I held this routine for months before I left for the army.The closer it got to be leaving for basic training however anxiety came back, I was surprised by it more than anything I felt I had grown past that feeling but the doubt crept in. How did I know what was best for me if I had made all these mistakes before, I asked myself. I would tell myself it would be the best thing to happen to me, that I needed to try for myself before I would know for sure. I had no plan B either and I had came to the end of my parents patience with being unemployed. The night before I was set to leave my worries had became to much for me and I woke my dad in the middle of the night to ask for advice, my voice was trembling as I told him my doubts and fears around going. What if your all right and I can't do it. His voice calmed me enough to where I really listened to what he had to say. He told me that he would miss me but that if I had wanted to do it before then I had to see if I was right otherwise I'd ask myself for the rest of my life if it was the right choice, "you, can always come back" were the words that settled me enough to get some sleep. I thought its just nerves they'll be gone when I get there.

I was in the army for the grant total of one week. I don't want to speak badly about the army itself as I still admire those who make careers out of it and the ones who want to serve for their country, but it wasn't for me. It made me feel trapped as soon as I got there, I missed the familiarity of home and the thought of not being able to see my family for a long time. The shock of the changes that were going to happen if I stayed gave me the most horrendous anxiety I have ever experienced, but almost simultaneously valuable epiphanies for how I wanted to live my life. I wanted freedom more than anything, to be able to be in charge of my own life. That what little family I had left was worth spending time with while I still could, I wanted my own ideas and visions to be listened to and manifested. I lasted to the second day before I told the Sargent I wanted to leave. The problem with this was I had said the oath and became a training soldier I was no longer a civilian and if I was to leave it would be considered treason. Again I found myself in a mess I had made for myself, I had no

idea how I was going to get out of this. The teachings from the secret and the power of visualisation was all I had to feel some sense
of control of my situation. I didn't know if I was going to have to
stay for the first 6 weeks before we went on leave or if I refused to
do the tasks would they put me in military jail, which was completely possible. It was actually made crystal clear thats exactly
what would happen if I became detremental to the other recruits
training. I had no desire to cause trouble I just wanted out. I wrote
what was important to me as it came to me in the few days before
they told me what was going to happen to me. I remember phoning my mum and my girlfriend from the bathroom and fighting
back tears telling them I had made a big mistake coming here. I
felt stupid, like I'd let everyone down and I was returning with
nothing and only had myself to blame. To stop the internal bat-
tering I was giving myself, I focused on manifesting a way out, a
way out of the mind-set came from writing my affirmations.
Things like having the freedom to work for myself, and enjoying
life more and not taking my life for granted. Having a purpose
that was worth living for. I was desperate for another chance at
finding a place that really suited me. I also manifested a way out
that didn't cause me to commit treason. We had to sign off our
medical examinations to be able to continue with the training. It
was at our digression to sign and it was made clear that if we
didn't sign it we would have to go back to civilian life. This was
my way out.

As I sat on that plane home, with my newly shaved haircut
courtesy of the British army. I knew I was facing an uncomfortable time, I had to stop trying to run and start to crawl. I felt
disappointed as I had spent time looking at other careers and not
found anything that had ticked as many boxes as the army did.
As I predicted my dad made me go back to the job centre the following day. That night I was desperate, I knew I could manifest a
job using the law of attraction, if I had managed to get out of the
situation I was in a few days ago. I envisioned walking in and them
giving me a job straight away. I needed this, my dad had reached
the end of his patience. I wanted it as well, being employed by

anyone was better than just daydreaming about working for myself. I was in the job centre for all of half an hour before they told me to go to this cafe around the corner and ask for a job. I got a job washing dishes in this cafe. It was a start. I didn't let myself feel embarrassed about this as I knew I had attracted the job and it must lead somewhere better. Within the first week the owner had asked for the catering college to come speak to me. He would receive grants from the government if I was in part time education, and I would gain a useful qualification that would give me a career. I couldn't believe my luck, I had played about with the idea of being a chef on and off through the years, watching my mum cook, as a child. My imagination ran wild with this, I could be a fitness chef eventually I could be the next Gordon Ramsey he was pretty wealthy. It also gave me a sense of pride when I thought about telling people I was a chef when they asked what I did. It grew on me quickly and the depression of failing at the army and letting my family down subsided. I phoned my mum, dad and girlfriend as soon as I had signed up for college. I was relieved more than anything, it felt like the spotlight was off me. I could answer truthfully what I was doing with my life. Two years lay ahead of me, at college to get a qualification that would be recognised across the world and gave me the opportunity, if I persisted, to travel and cook anywhere. At the very least it would be a fall back career for me.

College was only one day a week through in Motherwell, I was still getting used to living in Glasgow, I had spent most of my time there so far unemployed and in the house. I met one of the other students at the train station on my first day. He would become a close friend and still is to this day. I hadn't realised how much I had missed being social, I found my voice again. Making sure this time I stayed true to myself, I wanted friends who liked me for me this time. The college work itself was easy, the adult vocabulary used by the teacher and us made it feel nothing like school. Which I was relieved by, there was about six other boys my age and we developed a good friendship throughout our training. The first year we would go where you would expect a group of apprentice chefs to go at lunch, McDonalds, which we still laugh about. I looked forward to college and seeing everyone, work was okay too, as I knew it was a means to an end I could bare the belittlement of my ego in being a dishwasher. After a few months of this routine I was fired from the cafe for leaving dishes in the sink. I felt it was brutally unfair as I had finished my shift and someone was coming in to take over my station. I think it was more because they were struggling financially and couldn't afford to keep paying me. Either way I panicked, I didn't want to lose my place at college or disappoint my mum and dad again. I was fired on the Friday and I had got a new job by Monday. I wasted no time phoning everywhere I could think of and asking for a job. In the end it was my girlfriends, at the time, cousin who worked as a chef in the local restaurant, back in the town my mum lived in who gave me the job.

This would change a lot unexpectedly, I was now spending a lot more time back in the town I had happily avoided due to my drinking and drug habits. To help me out her mum and dad let me stay whenever I was working and she would even drive me to work. I'm ashamed to admit I kept the relationship going longer than I wanted to because I needed the support. I didn't want to stay with my mum as she had her new man there and we would often argue if we spent too much time together. It also meant I seen my dad less, which always played on my mind as I worked, I soothed myself with the thoughts that this was going to help us both in the long run. I did see my friends in the town from time to time but I didn't touch any drugs other than a joint every now and then. The work was brutal, I had went from a 40 seater quiet cafe to a 150 seated busy restaurant. The 12 hour shifts and lack of pride in my work was an internal battle daily, I wanted to walk out every time the dishes were piled up to my ears and I had hours left of my shift. I was also not going home after work, I was going to my girlfriends where I felt like a visitor and this made me irritable not having any space to myself. I struggled with knowing it was what I had to do to stay in college but it was damaging my health. I was smoking cigarettes again for some kind of break at work and drink a few beers every night to help me sleep in a home I didn't want to be in. I was so thankful to her parents for letting me stay but this girl had her own problems that caused us to argue and increase the weight I felt I was carrying. I also had no time to train, no gyms were open when I finished work, not that I had the energy to do so. My diet wasn't great either as it would be whatever the chefs cooked that day for me I had little say, until I decided to just cook for myself when it was quiet. I had been enjoying the buzz of a busy restaurant on better days and couldn't wait to be a chef I was cooking every chance I had watching food programs and learning as much as I could.

Eventually the monotonous nature of washing dishes sixty hours a week had lead me to walking out. I finished my shift, explained I wouldn't be back and left. I had to get another job as soon as possible for college and my best friend from college gave me another opportunity. He worked for a big chain of restaurants that were always looking for staff. I lied and said I had been a commis chef before and got a job back in Glasgow, walking distance from the flat with my dad. This was a huge step forward for me, I felt proud going into work. At the time the restaurant was in the top 10 in Glasgow and all the chefs had been there a long time.I couldn't believe my luck. I absorbed all I possibly could from these chefs. A larder chef who had been there for 11 years taught me how he ran that section and I quickly learned to be as competent as he was in no time. I loved the job, it paid me a decent wage for the first time since leaving the lab. I was gaining experience of how restaurants work and how to cook pretty much everything I ever wanted to eat. It gave me freedom to express myself through dishes and develop the artistic side I had forgotten about for so long. It was also in Glasgow and there were 24 hour gyms near me, that's when I started training again. My love for training came back almost instantaneously, I had become closer with the boy from college and we started going to the gym together. After a 12 hour shift in a hot kitchen we took great pride in going to the gym and working out, when all the other chefs went home or went to the pub. We would watch the same fitness youtubers and talk about them and try out their workouts. I started to see a future I wasn't scared of, I felt confident that things would work out if I kept working and getting better. In my second year of college, I could see we had come on a great deal as chefs but due to working so many hours through the week we no longer paid any attention to what was being taught. We had done most of it before and so we saw the day at college as a day off from work more than a day to develop skills. Our lunch time McDonalds was exchanged for a pint or two in the local Weatherspoon's. Alcohol and chefs have always gone hand in hand, the stories we were being told week in and week out by our co-workers were seen as a right of passage. That we worked hard and partied and drank harder, as if the buzz of a busy service was it's own drug for us. The lifestyle lent itself to searching for a rush else where on days off and when the adrenaline wore off. I started to see an old side of me emerge. I enjoyed drinking when it was social and we perhaps took it too far now and again. I was still training however so I didn't feel as much of a waste of space as I should have, when I was drunk at 4 in the afternoon on a Wednesday with the other apprentice chefs. We had a great time passing the course and celebrating with a blow out, again my earlier experiences with drugs allowed me to be around people taking it and not participate. After a few months more of being a full time chef, now fully qualified. I continued to train after work I was putting in 14-16 hour days by the time I'd got home from the gym each night. The harsh reality of chef life began to take a toll. On one hand it felt good to get so much done in a single day. I felt like I was working hard, it seemed obvious to me that I should be working this hard, is that not what everyone did? I found more peace at that pace it didn't allow much free mental space to think about the things that scared me, the endless "what if" thoughts that roamed my mind when my body stopped. What if this is the best I can be? What if this isn't going to end well? What if I start drinking again? My problems outside of the kitchen didn't torment me day in and day out and end with a binge in alcohol if I kept the foot down on training and work. Because I knew it would spiral me into a dark place where it would become harder to work and in turn the uncomfortable thoughts would trickle back in.

They came instead with dramatic burn out and anxiety attacks. I was so engrossed in working to somehow make up for my earlier years that I ignored fatigue and signs of depression. I had worked for two years and only took one holiday with my girlfriend after she made me take a break. It had gotten to a point where I would ignore how I was feeling and work through it. One night in the kitchen we were just ticking over. I had become competent enough to do what was asked of me but I was struggling. Physically I could not catch my breath even when I stopped. I kept putting it down to this cold I had been fighting. Thankfully eventually I finished the shift. It wasn't until I got home that night that my girlfriend said we should go to A&E. My dad was sleeping by the time I got home so I didn't wake him. At the hospital they rolled their eyes when I told them I had been working, as if it can't be that bad if you went to work. After some tests the doctor sat down with me and told me he was surprised I was still conscious. I had developed pneumonia in my left lung and my oxygen levels were drastically lower than they should be. They gave me intravenous antibiotics and a breathing mask and told me if my oxygen levels didn't improve I would be kept in overnight. To my confusion even though my levels went back up they told me I wasn't to work for a week and longer if it didn't improve.

I don't say this to say look how tough I am or that I'm special compared to anyone else, I say it to show just how strong your emotions can be. It wasn't that I wanted to work because I loved my job more than life .I
t was that how I felt about my life and where I was, was too much to accept, I avoided how I was still feeling, lost, scared and insignificant. Work ethic had never been an issue for me it came in boat loads from both sides of my family, I don't think in my life I've seen my mum stay still for more than an hour unless she was unwell or with the broken ankle lovingly given by our family pet. My dad had been working since he was 15 and he was pushing 70 and showed no sign of even slowing down. It wasn't that I

was just working too hard I neglected looking after myself properly, I didn't give myself time when I had it. I was so exhausted on days off that for a long time I wanted to leave my girlfriend but couldn't build up the energy to face the emotional connotations with it.

The week the doctors told me to have off was hard. I couldn't drink as I was on strong antibiotics and I couldn't train as my respiratory system couldn't cope, I would get so out of breath just climbing stairs that my vision would get blurred. I visited my mum like most people when they're not well, my mum being a counsellor was the most valuable asset to me growing up. She explained that when you ignore the signals to slow down that life will make you eventually. This might be quite spiritual for some readers and may come as a shock but there was always some belief in me that something more powerful than me was involved in life. It was comforting because I understood it in my own way, law of attraction supported it as well. I felt fatigued and ignored it therefore the result of that showed up in my reality. A week of looking after myself and slowing everything down began to clear some of the mental fog I had been living in. I still felt to a degree less than I thought I should be, although when said out loud being chef in a high class restaurant at only 20 sounded good. It fulfilled my desire to be proud when people asked me what I did for a living. I was being creative and working with my hands I had developed skills that were usefull and not just something everyone can do. It allowed me to live, from the outside atleast, a desireable lifestyle. The reality however was a lot of grunge work, peeling potatoes and emptying bins that didn't fill me with pride. Things I feel do have a place in development but after a while doing these jobs day in and day out naturally drove me to wanting more. It also made me look at the entrepreneurs I had always followed and ask myself, why I wasn't moving towards that. I really assessed where I was unhappy in my career and in my life, again revisiting the painful times in my life where I felt insignificant and betrayed by friends and my own expectations of how life should have been. I had to forgive myself and those I feel wronged me. I had to say goodbye properly to the friends I just didn't see again, they still played on my mind.

I had to break up with my girlfriend it was going nowhere and we didn't have much happiness. I had to hug my dad and remember not to take it for granted, him getting older was getting harder to face every day. I had to build a relationship with my mum after our early disagreements that I hadn't completely made peace with. This was what I had been avoiding. If facing all of this was going to stop me ending up in the hospital again it would be worth it. Jeopardising all my hard work pretending nothing bothered me only showing this hard outer shell I had created.

It was easy to appreciate my parents consciously, my dad was one of my favourite people in every sense, still is to this day, I have never seen on movies or in real life someone I looked up to more. He like my mum was over spilling with knowledge and experience. We had managed to get away together the year we had moved to Glasgow, in autumn to Cyprus for a week. It was just the two of us and in that week there were no two conversations the same. He would walk out to this restaurant bar every morning we were there and watch the boats coming in. I would wake at the same time just get a workout in before running along to meet him. We spoke about everything, family and how he met my mum. His family before us and his relationships with his friends, who he had been meeting every Thursday for over 50 years. He had travelled most of the world and had stories about anything I chose to ask him about.

My mum is the closest thing to a saint I ever thought could exist. Her whole life was around helping others, from her seemingly heartless mother she didn't let that turn her bitter. I could go to her and tell her anything and she would listen and do her best to help without being cold and professional but with acceptance that she didn't have all the answers and would always help me find my own advice. Not only did our family and friends benefit from her sheer existence. She had also worked with people through rehab, divorces, post-natal depression, grief, prison and trauma of all kinds. She still put her heart and soul into her job because she makes a difference. She now supervises and mentors new counsellors passing on her vast knowledge and experiences to the next generation. She has impacted the world in such a selfless and positive way that my words here will never do her justice.

Again my family became my immediate support group, I also grew the friendship with my friend from college. We had been training together for a long time now and we had similar outlooks on life and fitness. He was a couple years younger than me and I took the lead in the gym but his nature was unmatched I learned a lot from how he was with people, talkative to everyone. He was naturally confident said things how he seen them and was effortlessly funny. He was always there for me through the whole journey of becoming a chef. No one else could have known me better we spoke for hours about what we wanted out of life and what we were going to accomplish. Even my dad had got so fond of seeing him he would often go sit with my dad in the flat while I finished work or whatever I was doing before we had planned to meet. You learn a lot about a person when they are struggling, not just in the gym during a hard set and the strain and determination cannot be masked from their face,but more than that he had his own family and relationship dynamics that he was coming to terms with as he grew and it was great to see those changes in someone other than myself, I know that those late night sessions where we pushed each other with no one else watching made a connection between us that is hard to explain. He is in every sense of the word my brother.

To ensure I wouldn't go back down the road of avoidance and working myself to burn out I had to have something else to focus on. Something bigger than me, a purpose that would keep me going through the hard shifts and late night gym sessions. It was sitting in the cricket field on a sunny day off with my friend from college doing what we always did on the very rare occasion we had the day off together, drinking playing music and talking. It was here that something that had only whispered at me before was given a name. Balanced Dreamers. If your reading this because you follow my business then you know all about this but for those of you who don't. I believe these two words represent my purpose in life. My love for fitness and training had been the one consistently happy thing I'd done throughout my life. I knew others were making great careers out of becoming personal trainers and building fitness businesses like gyms, meal prep companies, gym wear brands and supplements. The thought behind it was to have all the things that interested me in one place, one platform to direct all my efforts and hopefully help as many people as I could along the way. At the start we were passionate but had no idea what to do with that passion. We started the Instagram page and made a few posts, with very little feedback we quickly became discouraged. I resented the shallowness of people on social media, the materialistic people got liked and shared more than people with a genuine message to share. But I had felt so close to the answer that I kept at it and over the years it's clear to see from the business page when we were invested and when life got in the way.

Going back to work I had a different approach too. I had progressed 10 fold in the kitchen and I could now do all sections, I wanted what I thought I was worth. The thing was I was the youngest by 5 years and everyone had been there longer, there wasn't much space for me to progress. I went to the head chef about a raise stating that I could now run several sections and that my wage needed to justify that. He agreed I had improved but that I was already getting more than minimum wage for my age and he could only offer me another 30 pence per hour. It was enough to stem my frustrations for another few months. It was disappointing to realise that although I had got my qualifications and improved a lot, that it ultimately didn't get any further towards being financially secure, or living the life I envisioned for myself.

With being a chef my only viable option for work I kept going, finding pride in the work and trying to stay optimistic about progressing. I also moved forward with Balanced, I had invested what little money I had in getting my personal training qualifications. I had hours of course work to read and go through but it gave me a purpose. I didn't feel completely trapped by my job this way I could make a living for myself as well as being a chef and that would bring balance to my life. Yet again my head was back in the game, I daydreamed and visualised how it was all going to work. I saw myself as a personal trainer. I would finish my shift and on days I didn't want to train I had this saying that I would repeat the full way to the gym. "You've spent all day working for someone else, this work is for you". That saying still touches a very raw part of me and it pushed me through some hard days. The progress on the workbooks was slow, what little time I found to spend on them I struggled to keep motivated. I was tired in every way. I had built more pressure for myself instead of dealing with the stress I had, in a better way. When I did manage to sit down and do the work it would come naturally to me, I had spent so long watching fitness videos that I understood the vocabulary and had a better understanding of the physiology than I thought. I was working hard but I was happy, I was satisfied with myself for the first time in a long time.

My dad had turned 70 that summer, with me entering my twenties a few days before. He had reduced his work week down to 4 days and was at home more. He spoke to me about the rent saying that if he was to retire in the next year or so we might need to look for somewhere cheaper. I was confused by this, how could someone who had worked for nearly 50 years not be able to afford the rent in a two bedroom flat with his savings and pension. I had been paying digs for nearly 5 years too, I couldn't understand. He broke the math down for me and I could see what we would be short each month if he was to fully retire. I told myself I would make the difference. He had looked after me for 20 years I could step up and look after him now. I was still nowhere near making the money I needed and as much as I spun the wheel of working and doing my PT it wasn't going to be enough. I had noticed the same expression on my dad's face when he spoke about money as he'd had several times growing up. He stressed and worried about money, seeing this motivated me to work harder and earn as much as possible but it wasn't from a balanced state. It was pressured, by me, to live up to the ego I had for my life. This wasn't something I had ever had to worry about before. Along with the realisation of how little I was getting paid in comparison of what I wanted to do with it, this left me deflated and angry with life.

I noticed my patience deteriorate. I was under pressure that only I had created, I resented my work. I thought about the conversation about my wages, they don't care about me, I'm just another number to them. I felt the same about my dad's work, he had gave them years of service and never missed a day. Did loyalty mean nothing? It was a hard lesson I'm sure a lot of people face. That until you take your career and income into your own hands you're a slave to the man, excuse the cliché teenage quote.

My days off were often spent drinking with my friend and trying to think of ideas for Balanced that would make us some extra income, the frustration I once felt as a teenager was the same, particularly when I drank. I would get to a point where I was so exhausted and fed up of working with nothing to show for it that I felt, just let the world burn. What's the point anyway I could work for the next 40 years and still be in my dad's position, I could feel myself slipping back into depression I was becoming desperate for a change. I just wanted something to go my way.

Despite my best efforts my dad couldn't retire. He left the lab as they could no longer afford his wage, whilst only working part time.

This didn't stop him though and at 70 years old he got another job working as a personal shopper in a supermarket. My heart broke for him, he had gave his entire working life to being a dental technician and they couldn't allow him to retire with his dignity due to their own greed. I was angry at the world, I wanted to change things for us and I worked 6 days a week 14-16 hour days,' week in week out. Eventually my dad decided to retire, the job wasn't worth the hours and effort for him he was getting up so early that his aging body just didn't want to listen to him he deserved to enjoy the last of the money he had from selling the house, and if that meant moving we would have to start looking in the next few weeks. He told me it wasn't my fault and that he didn't expect me to pay any more than I already was,but it felt like I had let him down. I felt shame and was embarrassed with myself, I hadn't been able to support him but I knew he wasn't hurt by this, he accepted it. He had travelled most of the world and enjoyed his money when he had it. He wouldn't have changed anything and this gave me some relief. I understand as I write this that the pressure and stress I had was caused by me, I set unrealistic goals and achievements for myself and expected them to happen overnight. I turned to alcohol to blow off steam and slow down the thoughts that caused me to feel this way. But it was self-inflicted, I was constantly behind my expectations which made me feel worse. I didn't pat myself on the back once even after 80+ hour weeks. I still had this fear that who I had been when I was taking drugs and had no direction was going to come back if I stopped or slowed down. The pneumonia scare had been forgotten about, if I can't achieve what I wanted I thought, "What is the point in being alive anyway". As silly as it sounds to me now this was my mind set, I was blind to the good in my life. In constant pursuit of more. I would get to a point quite often when I drank where I felt like I was doing damage, either physically or to my self esteem, and I'd drink quicker or buy more to silence those thoughts. I was trying to run away from the noise in my mind. The constant unanswerable questions. This was vividly becoming a slippery slope for me as on occasion I would wake up somewhere I didn't recognise and be almost angry I'd woken up at all. As brutal as this may be for the people who love me to read, I was in those moments completely ignorant to my life.

I returned again to the law of attraction, I meditated and focused on letting go and being in harmony with the world around me. I had lifted the pressure off from the gym a little and had stopped working as much as I possibly could. We had to move anyway there was less pressure to change that now, I had some breathing space for another couple of months. I got a good portion of my studying done and felt more in control of the anger and depression. I set new goals, pass my driving test, finish my tattoos, ended the relationship with the girlfriend, there was little she could do or say to persuade me otherwise. I had drifted apart from her over time and I should of left long before I did. She was amazing in her own right but we were not good together. I knew that if all I achieved that day was looking after myself and went to the gym it was far better than numbing myself with alcohol. The people I looked up to made it look effortless, as though the world changed for them. I was trying to force change and created more resistance from it. I was trying to let off the gas and just be the 20 year old I was, who didn't have all the answers.

I came home early from work one evening to the same flat as before, we hadn't moved yet, and was surprised to find my dad in bed already. I went in as I often did and told him I was home. He spoke in broken sentences about not feeling great and had went to bed early. I put his speech down to him being tired and went to bed myself. The next morning I had asked my girlfriend to come round as I was going to speak to her about our relationship. My dad came in the living room and tried to say good morning. The conversation that ensued didn't make much sense, he seemed tired and confused. With no thought of it being anything serious we had a laugh about it and he said he was going to bed to sleep it off. I let my girlfriend go to work without speaking to her, my mind was with my dad. I phoned my mum and told her about the conversation as it was playing on my mind. She told me that it was possible he had had a stroke. I felt as though a train had just hit my chest, surely that's not the case. I said that I would keep an eye on him and take him to the hospital if he was still the same when he woke up.

My mind wouldn't quiet, I phoned my brother who was at the university along the road. He said he would be there after his lecture and see what he thought. I didn't know what to do, if I should wake him up and just phone a taxi and go to the hospital with him, or let him sleep. The part of me that didn't want to believe this was happening told me to let him sleep. I thought there's a possibility he will wake up fine and I was holding everything onto that. I did what I always did when I had thoughts I didn't like, I numbed them with alcohol. I had phoned my best friend from college that knew my dad and he came round to wait on my brother with me. As it often did speaking to him gave me an outlet to better understand my thoughts and as I realised that this could be serious I started to get upset. I tried to hide my tears from my friend but he knew me too well and just came and gave me a hug without saying anything. It was one of the first times a friend has actually been there for me and didn't judge me for having emotions. People ask me today why he's still my best friend, I tell them I love him as much as I love my family. My family to me was my mum, my brother, my dad and me. He is as important to me.To know me well enough and not judge my emotions just to be there for me.

My brother arrived a couple hours later. He woke my dad up and decided straight away that we would go to the hospital. He phoned his girlfriend who was in the area and she drove us there. My dad didn't speak as he knew it might worry us but he looked scared and I knew he didn't want to go. I struggled not to cry, I was worried, I had spent my whole life with him. We had often spoke about his death as cold as it sounds, he wanted to make us more comfortable with it knowing with his age we might not be adults by the time he passed. We knew he didn't want to be kept alive artificially, he would say just let me go. If I start talking nonsense just take me out and put me out my misery I don't want to be one of those old people he would say jokingly. We had spoken about it before but he was remarkably fit and healthy it didn't cross my mind that it could be anytime soon. He often joked when he did eventually go to the doctors for a checkup that they would ask for his medical records and he would have to explain that he didn't have any and that the last time he had been in the hospital was when he had been born. Even then he had been born in their house and taken to the hospital afterwards so they could sign the birth certificate.

It didn't take long for the doctor to confirm he had had a stroke. He would be kept in for a few days so they could do some tests and check the severity of it. He nodded and agreed when he could but struggled to say a sentence that made any sense. He even tried to walk us to the door of the hospital as I could see he wanted to say to us it's okay. It was hard to leave him, he had almost, overnight, started to look his age. He was in the hospital for a week to rest. They explained to us that the stroke had really only affected his speech and that physically he was safe to come home. The nurses who had looked after him were sad to see him leave, despite his lack of speech he was more animated with his facial expressions and was still making people laugh. Doing the physio therapy tests he had squeezed the nurses hands to check his grip. With him having worked with his hands for so long his grip was almost vice like. He took great pleasure in squeezing the nurses' hand and showing that he was still strong, to the nurses' surprise.

At home I couldn't pretend nothing had happened. I didn't know it at the time but I had had my last conversation with my dad. Simple communication became time consuming, I tried not to show him how scared I was when he would say something that made no sense. He had a speech therapist come to the house a few times but there didn't seem to be much improvement. Despite his stroke he didn't stop going out, he would ask a word or two he thought he might get stuck at before he went and took some cards to show people if he was struggling. He stayed positive for the majority of the time but there was occasions where he would get upset with himself as he couldn't think of a word, when he cried I felt my heart break more. There was nothing anyone could do, my brother who was nearly qualified as a lawyer made sure we had power of attorney and we looked for ways to move my dad closer to family. His big sister (nana) had been a nurse before her retirement and was a comfort to him through this time, despite my feelings of her she knew more than I did and my dad seemed to feel better with her being there. I had spoken to my work about my situation and they agreed to give me whatever I needed. I used work as an escape, I put my head down became quiet and just done the job. Two months after my dad's stroke he was more capable of being himself at home, at least while we made other arrangements. I had all but forgot about my studying, I focused again on making money. I asked for my raise again as I was desperate, again they told me no. I grudged every minute I spent from then on working there. My patience was pushed over the edge one shift where I had come in on the later start, to be told the guy I was supposed to be running the section with was running late. I couldn't hide my disgust as the head chef told me we were changing the whole menu that day, as he showed me the prep list. Added to the fact that the list was twice as long as I'd ever seen it, he also ended the discussion by saying that the chef who was late was now cdp of the section. This meant he was my senior and above me. This chef had come in countless times still drunk from the night before, late on several occasions and was lazy with his prep work. I could not believe it. I had been working for that promotion, I knew I was a better chef and that I worked harder than he did. To face the reality of this chef being my superior was something I couldn't swallow. As he came in clearly hungover from the glazed look in his eyes I had had enough.

My first response was to punch the chef like I had the bully in the lab but I knew that wasn't right. The sheer unjust nature of the world surrounding me was too much to do nothing, I fought with myself trying to work out what to do. I got changed out of my whites without saying anything, I said goodbye to some of the chefs I liked and I walked out. The head chef stopped me on my way out an asked where I was going, I simply said I'm away. With the shock in his face painting a thousand curse words I said, "If you think that chefs work is more valuable than mine then I don't want to work under you". I said it as calmly as I could, I wanted to be heard for what I was saying not reacted to because of my tone. From there I left and slowly walked home, how had it came to this again. I had put hours and hours into that place, I had learned as much as I could, I covered people's shifts, I was always on time and left my section clean. I felt I had done everything I could have done. I didn't have to tell my dad, he would just worry about me and that's the last thing he needed. I phoned another friend from college and got an interview for the following day. My dreams were on hold I needed an income that would get my dad whatever he needed, wither that was sheltered housing or carers I didn't care for myself this was about him.

I had actually gotten closer to my girlfriend during this time as she was there to ask me how I was coping and be someone for me to talk to. We still argued over things that seemed so insignificant to me that she would be hurt by my indifference. I was selfish in our relationship, I didn't know how to deal with everything that had happened and could happen to my dad. I wasn't even caring for myself let alone her at the time. I couldn't face ending it and losing a place to stay as I still didn't know what was going to happen. My plans of leaving her took a background position in my thoughts. I of course still spoke to my mum almost every day, she supported me from a distance while I came to terms with the inevitable changes. She said there was always a place at her house for me but I felt as though that was a step backwards. I had gotten used to having my own space and working the hours that I did, it didn't seem feasible to live 40 minutes away from work. Everything was up in the air all at once, I didn't know where I was going to live or where I was going to work, I felt everything was overwhelming. I couldn't control any of it I just had to wait and see what would happen. I turned to the only comfort I knew that wasn't damaging, the gym. For that hour or so when I was in the gym I was free from everything. It was time for me and my music, channelling my aggression into the weights. I would always feel emotional after a workout as though I had moved the anger and frustrations out of the way to reveal the real fear and sadness they stemmed from. It was therapeutic for me and without it I don't know how I would have coped.

Too many things had happened in my life to not trust that whatever happened was supposed to happen. That it was out of our control no matter what we did. I often remembered how I just jumped in a better direction and life let me land safely. Like when I left the job washing dishes, I believed something better would come from it. My dad's brother had died some years earlier and in the middle of the night my dad had woken suddenly and just knew he had to go see him. As he left the house and got in his car to go, my mum got a phone call from the family to say he had passed. A similar thing had happened to my mum. She had dreamed of comforting her mother and then the next day she was comforting her mother because her father had died suddenly. It's a sort of sixth sense that gives you a sign something is happening. In the old house once we built the garden there was always these two distinctively fat grey wood pigeons that would sit on the fence and use our bird feeder. These two birds were everywhere I went, we had moved to Glasgow where two more fat distinctive grey wood pigeons had made home in the trees in front of our window. On holiday they were often on the balcony even in climates I didn't know they had pigeons. Even later when I sat my driving test as I pulled out they were sitting on the grass right in the middle of the road, as if to say good luck. I know there not the same birds and to some this might sound like I've become completely insane. I don't fully understand the significance of them, they just seem to be everywhere I am when I feel alone. They make me feel like I'm in the right place, that everything that's happened has lead me to where I am now. They were, in my mind at least, a sign that I wasn't alone. That god or whatever higher power you want was letting me know that everything happens for a reason. I'm sure I'm not the only one with strange sensations and attachments to things that make them feel as though there's something bigger than us out there.

I got the job in the new restaurant, my friend from college had set up, with the increase in wages I had been asking for in my previous position. The pleasure of signing the contract was dulled by the situation at home though. It no longer felt significant to me and although it was once what I wanted I quickly found more things to want for. It didn't change the fact I couldn't have a conversation with my dad or take control of what was going to happen. I enjoyed the change in work place, new faces and dishes that made the days go quicker. The friend who had got me the interview was the junior sous. This made it light work, learning the dishes and working with someone who I was genuinely close with. Reminiscing about college and nights out we'd had together made the long shifts feel shorter. I also felt valued more in this restaurant, the increase in volume of customers each night moved me further forward as a chef. It was a different challenge, which I embraced. I also started a great relationship with the head chef as we were similar in our approach to the job, he didn't take himself too seriously and would have a laugh as long as the work was being done well. Things were feeling somewhat normal again, I enjoyed my work. My dad was still capable of doing everything he used to now, meeting friends, cooking and walking almost every day. It did however stop him reading which left him without his favourite vice, he was always behind a paper on his chair with his can of Stella poured into a wine glass. His stroke had changed his taste buds to where he no longer enjoyed Stella, a beer he had been drinking for years. Which was funny in its irony he joked he always drank responsibly and this was how he'd been repaid. He seemed to take it all in his stride he never looked depressed or sorry for himself he just got on with life.

Three months later I was enjoying a long lie as I was on the late shift. I was woken up by a bang, as if furniture had been getting moved down stairs. I got up and went through to my dad's room. He wasn't there, this wasn't unusual he was always up earlier than me and I assumed it was nothing. I phoned him just to make sure and was surprised to hear the phone ring from his bedroom. As I walk back in the room I notice his bed hadn't been made, this was really not like him. The blinds were also still shut, with my panic rising slightly I moved around the room to open the blinds. It was then I found my dad, on the floor next to his bed. He had taken another stroke in the night and when he tried to get up to go to the bathroom he had realised his right leg wasn't working. I asked if he was okay as I picked him up and lay him on his bed, but he didn't answer. I realised he was trying to respond but couldn't. It's hard to put myself back in that position and really, to describing the feelings, I couldn't do it any justice. If you have ever lost a parent and had to watch them deteriorate in front of you with nothing you can do to change it, my heart goes out to you.

After phoning the ambulance I called my brother, he was there before the ambulance. All I said was "its dad" he replied with "I'm on my way". I admired my brothers' ability to deal with things logically, he had known what he wanted to be since school and went out and got it. He always was my motivation to be better I felt comfortable knowing he was there with me, he stayed strong. Through the first stroke he stepped up and done the right thing with the power of attorney and everything he could with almost no emotion. But even he shed a tear as they put my dad in the ambulance on a wheelchair.

Not a lot changed straight away, we knew even if it wasn't immediate that my dad's time with us was limited. He had always said this was the situation he didn't want to be in, helpless and unable to look after himself. He was given the strongest antidepressants they had but still, with vague communication we knew he wasn't happy. Our lives began to circle around visits to the hospital to see him. Despite having a serious stroke he always lit up when we walked in, it was devastating to watch my once quick witted humorous healthy father become a shell of who he once was. I remember holding his hand in the ward and seeing all the scars I knew every story behind. Making sure to remember as much as I could about him. He would later be moved to a unit of the hospital with people his age with similar health conditions. His stroke had been severe but he was now stable, we tried to go back to work and find some sort of normality but my head was constantly filled with doubts about the future and what to do next. I've later learned that your body tends to numb you in situations like this, to protect you in a way. I remember being able to continue and find some peace in my work. Despite everything that was going on with my dad circumstances in the kitchen had changed and I was offered my friends' earlier junior sous position, as he was leaving. Having built a good relationship with the head chef and him being so understanding of me needing time off and different things to make seeing my dad easier I took the position happily. The promotion meant that for the first time in my life money wasn't my immediate concern. I took great pride telling my dad I had got the job, I don't know how much he understood but I let him know he didn't have to worry about anything other than his health.

My dad would sadly die a few months later, surrounded by a few close family members and myself. The time from his first stroke to this had only been 6 months. In a way I was grateful to have that time with him knowing his death could be any day. I got to say goodbye properly, I kissed his head and told him he had done everything he could for us and that I would see him again. That night while drowning my sorrows the sky became so beautiful that I'll never forget, it was as if god was telling me he had got there safe. Although my thoughts were with my dad I couldn't ignore the fact I had been left with nowhere to live. I had to pack up his flat and get rid of what I couldn't keep. I had no choice but to move in with my mum and her partner, a living situation I was looking for a way out of before I'd even unpacked. It wasn't that I didn't love my mum I just didn't want to be there. We were too alike and it was too much when I was grieving and didn't want to listen to reason. My brother done the majority of the funeral planning, we knew my dad wanted to be cremated. He didn't like the thought of us feeling inclined to visit his grave on special occasions, I want you to go live your own life he told us. That our memory of him was enough. I admired his strength to be so selfless, his bravery to choose to die from not taking the medication is something I don't know if I could do myself.

With my brother dealing with my dad's estate I had to sell his car to help pay for the funeral. My brother and I paid for the wake with help from my mum. My dad's twin brother flew over from South Africa to attend, he had been retired for 20 years and had a wealthy wife. They lived in a big gated community and had maids and gardeners to help tend to the pineapple trees in their garden. We didn't ask for help financially but he never thought to offer anything, same with his big sister. I wasn't angry at the time but the disgust that grew on me from this makes me still ignore his calls. Me and my brother vouched that wherever we found ourselves in the world if we got a call to say our brother needed us we would drop everything and be there. It reinforced my distrust for people, my dad would have done anything for him but his twin brother had only phoned to ask if we could change the date to better suit his flight. The circle of people around me I could trust had now fell to, my mum, my brother, and my close friend from college.

I done my best at the funeral to say goodbye but I was inconsolable, the humanist read what I had to say. I spoke of the holiday I mentioned in this book, of spending my whole life with him and never having the same conversation twice. I spoke honestly about feeling jealous of some of the people there on that day, knowing that I had only known him 22 years out of his 71. His first wife and one of their sons attended but I paid them no mind, they were no more or less the family that did attend. I found some peace in knowing he had a good life regardless of the seemingly abrupt ending. To my surprise my friends from the town had come to support me, it was a great comfort to have them sitting behind me. I had some hard days facing the grief as you would expect, not knowing what to do with myself. The thing with loosing someone so close to you, as my mum would later explain to me, is that your sense of self gets knocked. Each day you spend with them in your life you reinforce who you are to them and who they are to you. Without my dad I was "homeless" I had a place to stay but he had been home to me for the majority of my life, this left me restless for a long time. But no matter how depressed I got or drunk to the point I fell asleep on the pavement outside my girlfriend's house I knew it would pass. I had come too far to let this drag me back towards drinking and drugs that would be a disgrace to my dad.

As I always did, to control the emotions I ignored them, and went back to work after a week. He had died on the 3rd of June, a month with father's day, my birthday and his own birthday. As I turned 22 I chose to ignore the milestone and just spent it with my mum and my brother. After a couple months I had been feeling better at work, I travelled on the train from my mum's house to the gym, using the time to read over my personal training course. I would then work my 12 hour shift and get the train back. The days bled into each other, I didn't sleep well and felt like I was on autopilot. I had ended my relationship with my girlfriend finally as I no longer knew how to fake the affection so I was staying with my mum. Although I was making good money I still couldn't afford to live in Glasgow myself. The travel was taking up too much of my time. I didn't see a way out, I didn't want to change jobs again as I was enjoying where I was. My mum supported me with cooking and doing my washing through this time as every waking minute was spent working, travelling or studying.

My answer to where to live would come in the shape of a new waitress who had started at my work. She was timelessly gorgeous, I knew she liked me but I didn't know what I wanted at the time. After some playground flirting with olives being thrown across the pass at each other and the time I picked her up and walked up stairs with her on my back to put her in a bin. I was strong from the training I was doing and wanted to show her, I admit it. It worked however immature it may have been. She asked me quietly one day what was wrong with me. I didn't understand, she said well excuse me if I'm wrong here but you seem sad. Like your carrying something, I can see it. I was so stunned by this, how she saw through me like that. I had only ever heard my mum have empathy of that level, she looked at me differently. Our friendship grew as time passed and I started to look forward to seeing her at work. She was outgoing and always asked me to come for a drink with the other front of house staff after work. I allowed myself to go, she was like no one I had ever met before. She had wrote me a card after I had told her why I seemed sad, it just said that everything happens for a reason and that she was there for me if I needed to talk. My intuition was pointing all the signs to her, "everything happens for a reason" that was my belief and I hadn't told her that. Her nature was always to look after everyone around her, the closer we got we exchanged stories that had lead us there. Her relationship with her mum hadn't been easy, her dad wasn't in much of her life at all. We connected on a deeper level, there was an understanding between us that didn't need to be said. That I couldn't put in words if I tried. Circumstances had her going through a break up when we met and we both felt like we had nowhere to call home. After what felt like months we had sat too long in the pub and missed our last train home, she too stayed 40 minutes away with her parents, while her ex-boyfriend found somewhere to stay other than her flat. I suggested we get a hotel together, it wasn't for any other motive than we would both have somewhere to go. That night was easily the most intimate I had ever been with someone before. It felt like I'd known her my whole life, a level of affection I wasn't sure was real. The void left in my heart from losing my dad felt almost filled by this woman. We spent three months staying in hotels nearly every night, spending a fortune just to have a few hours in our bubble. It was effortless romance, I adored her very early in our relationship and I felt like it was mutual.

To give us both somewhere to stay we decided to move in together. We rationalised it by having a flat mate who we also worked with trying to keep it as casual as we could, understanding fully that we were in danger of moving too fast. We found a lovely modern flat in the west end of Glasgow, It was a dream we could afford it somewhat comfortably and it was a short train into town where we all worked. We worked hard to keep what we had, we spent so much time together that it felt strange being apart. In the beginning things that shouldn't matter started to build up. The mess of the flat would irritate me, I was used to everything being clean and in place at home and it caused some unnecessary arguments. It was minuet compared to the lifestyle we were now living though, we were drinking in lovely west end bars most nights. Eating out on days off and enjoying being together in every sense. Having that escape from reality together where we both had genuine care for each other allowed us to push through working long hours and we both got the opportunity to be promoted again. She was great at what she did, hospitality was something she actually enjoyed and took pride in. Unlike most people in the industry doing it because they couldn't find anything else. She learnt about wine and taught tasting sessions. She even got me to start enjoying white wine, something I would normally turn my nose up at the thought of. Her promotion was to a supervisor meaning she had some managerial control of the front of house staff. I was beyond pleased for her.

I had also been offered the sous chef role. The head chef had gone through a recent divorce and had left a lot more responsibilities to me. I had repaid the favour he had gave me when my dad was in hospital and we became a great team just the two of us. The current sous chef had left leaving only me as junior sous and the head chef to juggle the weekly workload normally split between three senior chefs. My new position would be the most money I had ever made, I would have more responsibilities and would be expected to cover the head chefs' day off. I was happy with who I worked with, I had recently moved into a flat with someone I loved dearly. It didn't take long for me to accept the position. Despite how quickly things had changed for the better for me, I didn't feel the same. There was still a numb feeling I couldn't locate, that had been there since watching my dad take his last breath. I carried it a lot easier as the grief of my dad ran its course but I knew it was in there somewhere. It hit me when I got the contract, I was opening it in the flat with an elated girlfriend proudly watching me. I became so emotional seeing the money and position of sous and my name next to it. I had been working as hard as I could in this field for 4 years and this was finally something to show for it. The emotion came from the realisation that hard work had paid off through all those hours spent peeling potatoes and washing dishes, I had been fucked over in my last restaurant and trusting myself had proved to me, I was as good as I thought I was. The thing was, the only person I wanted to tell was my dad. I had finally made enough to look after him, if this had only been a year earlier. My thoughts got away from me a little as I thought about it but ultimately I knew he would have been proud.

As I settled into the new position the stress levels of

running a 150 seater restaurant at 22 took a lot out of me. I was still one of the youngest in the kitchen and I was now second in charge. I had chefs older than me with more experience under my instruction and it became a balancing act to get the best out of them without portraying the image of an ignorant pre Madonna. This was helped drastically by the start of our new junior sous. He was the best chef I have ever worked with, still is, family issues had caused him to take a step back from high pressure roles and he took the junior sous responsibilities in his stride. He was a great teacher to me of how to communicate with my staff so that we worked as a team. Being a chef will teach you a lot about life if you look into it enough. There's often a therapeutic aspect of prep work, something as simple as chopping onions could become a deep point of peace for me even in the middle of a busy weekend shift. It teaches you patience that the more care and attention you put into your dish it's then rewarded in the eating experience. Of course no chef is truly good until he can handle the pressure, facing a daunting work load with little margin for era teaches you to take things one step at a time, as all steps are important to get the dish correct. Also on a social aspect a restaurant is often one of the most eclectic group of people you could create. We had ex-convicts as kitchen porters, people from all different countries who spoke different degrees of English, including a young Hungarian kitchen porter who we trained up to be a chef despite not being able to speak English. We had career driven employees and ones who were there just for a wage, all with their own stories and vocations. You learn quickly that there's no such thing as normal, as different as we all were when the restaurant got busy we all knew our jobs and the roles we played in the bigger picture. Something I returned back to several times to give me a more balanced perspective. To look at the big picture before deciding how to move forward. I had an apprentice start not long after and I took great pleasure in reliving the start of my career through him, I wouldn't shout or belittle him as I had been treated. I loved my new job, it gave me pride, a decent income and everyday was different. With the new income I bought whatever I wanted to be honest. I indulged in tattoos and clothes like they were nothing. I had become more creative by focusing on who I wanted to be and my tattoos were an outlet for that creativity. In a short period I tattooed my full back and dedicated one of my arms to a music geometric theme. Music had been another constant in my life that went hand in hand with my training, on days I felt I had no one to turn to, music would comfort me. The pain of tattoos was comforting to me, it stopped the focus being on the numbness I still felt. My days off were spent bouncing from bar to bar with either my girlfriend or my friends. I still worked out but my approach wasn't healthy, I was putting myself through brutal heavy sessions to then reward it by having a drink and eating pizza. I lost interest in cooking for myself having spent most of my week in a kitchen it was the last thing I wanted to do and I ate whatever was most convenient. I wasn't paying attention to my spending either just trying to chase that feeling of satisfaction from external things. My best friend had bumped into an old friend from college, who we had drifted from and we became close friends again. He opened up to us about his dad having passing recently. We shared some deep conversations about our experiences of losing a father and I felt he became someone I could trust almost immediately. He had a close friend that he brought into our circle, who I have now also grown to love as a brother. This boy has to be the most inspiring friend I have ever known, his upbringing seen him in horrendous situations and later into foster care. Yet he is kind and genuine with his friendship, he looks out for all of us as we all do. I've learnt a lot about resilience from this young man and admire him greatly. To hear more about him there will be a podcast where we discuss his life that I feel is worth its weight in gold for those of you feeling like the odds are stacked against them.These boys didn't care where I'd come from or what I had when we were out we were out as a team no one feeling the need to show off. We supported each other and shared in the small victories we all had individually as if they were our own. I grew to be comfortable showing my emotions with them, something I had never felt safe to do with friends before. I owe a lot of my growth and happiness from my times spent with these people and I make a point of letting them know that as much as I can. We had some great nights in my flat, having parties with everyone from work and just enjoying life with little thought of the future. I enjoyed having them there it felt more like home when I woke up and found them on the couch, being able to share what I was working hard for gave it real value.

My girlfriend and I booked a holiday to Portugal that summer and it turned out to be one of the most amazing weeks of my life, we strolled through the streets in the sun stopping for wine and meat boards, when the notion took us. Talking for hours about whatever came up, we planned a future together. I had great pride having her on my arm as we walked. Even at home we lived in a way that spoke deeply to me, we enjoyed the moment for what it was. I felt like wherever we went, as long as she was there I fit in. I felt at home. We had a saying that I feel sums up our relationship, we would often say this to each other when external things irritated us, "that this was our world, and everyone else was just in it." It wasn't that we didn't care about other people, in this time I had made the best friendships of my life and I cared deeply about the other people in my life. It was as though because we didn't have a lot of people before we met, both of us were from small families, that as long as we were together everything else would fall into place. It was a depth of love hard to express. She had Italian heritage, so she was fiery passionately standing up for something and it would often come out in her Ayrshire accent causing me to smile more than be intimidated, to her annoyance and irritation. She also had this cute vulnerable side where she would almost hide in my arms, I was protective over her which I knew was a tight rope. I learnt to love her for who she was, a socialite with lots of people wanting her time. I knew I had to let her have her own life and focus on what mattered to me. We often clashed as a result of reading each other wrong.

As time passed the honeymoon period had all but left us. We would argue as passionately as we done anything together. We spent a long time arguing and then talking things through and becoming closer and more understanding, but it was an exhausting way to live. I had let the stress of work get to me, we were drinking far too often and my health took a background position in my priorities. I was naive to the belief that the money I was making would make me happy. As the months passed and I kept buying whatever I wanted it never made me feel how I wanted it to. I learnt first-hand that money doesn't make you happy. The arguments between us had increased to the point we were both asking if it was worth it. I had built it up as just being stressed from work but she was worried about me. A few nights a week she would come home to me drinking and studying I would drink half a bottle of brandy like it was a couple of beers, I still enjoyed the numbing sensation it had on my thoughts and feelings. The problem was I wasn't sure what I was numbing. If I came home to an empty flat and instead of tackling the pile of dishes or washings, again I would escape behind my computer and work while drinking. I had everything I thought I ever wanted, money, a good job, a partner, a nice place to live and some real friends to share it with. I didn't know why I felt the way I did, that it didn't really matter.Nothing was breaking the cycle.This was my cycle, get what I want through working, realise it wasn't what I wanted, work to ignore the disappointment, reach breaking point, black out drunk, feel terrible, pledge to change and not do it again and be grateful for what I had, just to repeat it all again. I needed help and I wasn't going to be able to fix this with reading and youtube videos.

It wasn't intentional to go speak to my mum but me and my girlfriend visited to get a break from the flat and everything going on, it was still a very social flat with our flatmate being there and it was hard to find a sactuary together. My mum had moved out of my childhood home now and had married her partner in a lovely ceremony in that house before moving. We naturally came to the discussion about our constant arguing. It was eye opening to see just how easy it was to misinterpret each other. My girlfriend had PTSD from experiences before our relationship. This was triggered when I would sound angry or aggressive, causing her to be defensive, although my frustrations were never with her, I couldn't vocalise how I felt. In other words I thought I was telling her how I was feeling but I wasn't. This was enough for me to do something about it, I knew this was important, if I wanted to be heard in life.If I wanted to have healthy relationships, I was going to have to understand myself better in order to communicate with others. Following my mother's suggestion I enrolled in a COSCA counselling skills and communication course. She had also explained that I was still going through the grieving process and projecting my feelings of that in different areas of my life. The more I thought about this I knew she was right, I was still angry that I couldn't share any of my life with my dad. I didn't have motivation to do anything, I had forgot about Balanced Dreamers, I had traded my dreams for comfort. All the comfort had gave me was emptiness inside, every time I drank I had the same " let the world burn" mentality. I was being self-sabotaging without realising, and I was about to lose someone who gave me genuine happiness if I kept going.

The course would be taken at a counselling centre in Glasgow that my mum worked at, she also had a private practice so she was only part time there but well respected by the tutors taking the course. The first day I had psyched myself up enough that the discomfort didn't come until we were all sat in a circle doing an ice breaker. It dawned on me I really didn't feel confident speaking to new people, I was also one of the youngest there only one guy of a similar age who naturally I gravitated towards. The rest were all over thirties and apologies to any of those who are reading this but some were over 40. They had grown up jobs as well, a pastor, carers of all different descriptions and some looking to gain qualifications to help them with work. There was a real sense of everyone looking for some personal growth. I feared I had bitten off more than I could chew. The course was split into 4 sections with different counselling approaches and theories for each. It was expensive but it was something useful to finally spend my money on. The first module was mostly listening skills, I want to give the value of the course its own merit and I have done the essays on each section in painful detail. The overall learning from this section was that as much as people think they can communicate, that there was a huge difference from listening to respond and listening to understand. Something as simple as this straight away increased the harmony in my relationship. We slowed down to talk to each other again, I had countless epiphanies throughout the course that make me realise when I had been lazy in my communication skills and missed opportunities because of it. The thing with practicing counselling skills for me was that as I tried to put words to what I was feeling it made better sense to me than it did staying in my head. I see the value counselling and therapy can have on someone and I enjoyed the discomfort of continuing the course.

At work I had found a pace I could work without burning out too much, I felt comfortable delegating tasks instead of trying to do everything myself. There was a change in the head chef, he had started a new relationship and was taking more days off to spend with her, leaving me to deal with whatever jobs he'd chose to avoid. I launched new menus, adapted rotas as the staffs needs were getting ignored time and time again, and I even took the stock count on several occasions. A job that takes time to learn and I was left to deal with it. I understood he wanted to build his relationship but he had looked after only himself and it put unwarranted stress on me. I had decided that if I wanted to give this course my best efforts that I knew it needed. I would have to reduce my work load. I took my time with this decision, I loved the job but it didn't allow me to do much else with my life. Time was passing by quicker than I paid attention and unless I wanted to be stuck in this profession forever I had to make changes. As much as I enjoyed being a chef it was clear what my future could be. A lot of chefs I worked with didn't look after their health, they worked ridiculous hours and what relationships they had with partners didn't seem like what I wanted. I spoke with the head chef about stepping down from sous but continuing to work there while I finished my course. He was very understanding, at least that's what I thought. We agreed a time for me to step down that would allow him to find a replacement and it all seemed to have worked out for the best. We had discussed the change in pay that I was of course aware would be less than what I was making, but a fair hourly rate was enough to let me pay for my course and my flat. I knew the extra money didn't make me happy anyway and that if I could make that kind of money once I would be able to do it again. It wasn't until later that week that I stumbled across an email he had sent head office containing my contract. I opened it to see if it said anything about when my wages would change. I quickly went from curious to furious as I noticed he had taken even more money off our agreed rate and sent it through. I would now be paid minimum wage. I felt completely betrayed. After years of loyal work and helping each other, even building a relationship outside of work where we would catch up for a pint he had fucked me over.

  The timing of me finding this out fit perfectly with what we were learning about in the course. We were looking at Sigmund Freud's work the father of modern psychotherapy. His beliefs and teachings were focused how childhood and events in your past create your subconscious belief system that determines your behaviours and reactions. As well as how you handle any traumatic experiences. It was here I also learned the original meaning for the word "ego" Sigmund Freud had developed the idea that your ego was who you seen yourself as. Not just the cocky and arrogant connotations we gave the word but an honest view of yourself. It made sense to me why I had questioned my ego, I knew it was just who I believed I was and worked towards and this made me feel better. This almost confirmed a belief I'd had from years before. The betrayal of the head chef, a man I considered a friend, reminded me of the night my best friend turned on me and ended up phoning his dad on me. I couldn't believe it, I was devastated. I didn't understand why they both had treated me that way after everything we'd been through as friends. Ultimately their actions were theirs only, I didn't have to take responsibility for their distrust. I had to realise that this was part of life and that people when pushed will look after themselves first.

It may sound obvious to you but I wanted to trust people before this and always expected my loyalty to be reciprocated. I didn't let my anger make decisions for me this time, it had only led to more drama the last time, I was going to approach this differently. I went into work the next day with full intention of working the shift and bidding my time. As I sat in the changing room my head kept returning to the pain of the betrayal. My relationship with my girlfriend seemed to be one step forward and two steps back. I had tried to do so many things at once that I was getting nowhere fast. I knew everyone I had told had said to stay until I found something else and to play things safe but I couldn't do it. I couldn't bear the thought of looking back and thinking I done nothing about him walking all over me, what would my dad say if he was here. I went with the first response from my gut. Fuck him.

Luck would have it that the day I found out was also the day we had been paid. I was paid monthly and knew I could support myself for at the very most a month and a half on the wage along with savings I had. I walked in picked up my chef whites, the head chef was in doing the stocks and no one else was in. He didn't look at me as I had text him the night before asking if it was true and he had ignored it. He pretended to be on the phone out the front as I walked past him, I looked back stared him straight in the eyes and then smiled and gave him the finger as I walked across the road. Again as I write this I can hear the overwhelming judgement at the immaturity of myself, but it felt so good to walk away from it. From all of it the pressure to perform day in day out, the repetition of dish after dish after dish. It felt good to let go of something I felt was tearing my hands apart holding onto, to trust yet again that the universe will find a way for me.

My relationship had come to a point that we were going in circles. We had hurt each other unintentionally and we had no space to heal being together all the time. We agreed to move out and take time apart. If it was truly meant to be forever we trusted we would find each other again. It was the hardest break up I've ever been through. How we felt about each other hadn't changed, but for the sake of ever having a future together we had to move on. I would move back to my mums again and she would move in with a friend, leaving our flat mate to find her own way. I focused on my course as we spent some time apart for the first time since we had met nearly a year before. It doesn't sound like a long time but I cannot stress enough how much time we had spent together. We worked together, lived together and spent a lot of days off together. When I had finally moved into my mums and handed the keys back to the flat it really hit home how far, I felt, I had fallen. I had no job, I was living with my mum again at 22, I had lost what I thought was the love of my life, a friend I had been loyal to had threw me under the bus to save money and I had no idea how I was going to pay for the course. I remember feeling completely defeated. My mum had seen the change in me from being on the course and offered to pay the next module, provided I got myself a job and proved I wanted it. I got another job pretty quickly. Being a chef there's always work, it just depends on if the work is worth it or not. I had went from running a busy city centre restaurant doing 350-450 covers a night to a 30 seater hotel restaurant that was mostly lunch service and a fraction of the numbers. This suited me perfectly for the time being, although I felt a change in career was necessary I wasn't going to add that to "my to do list," I wanted to concentrate on the course. I missed seeing my friends as much but I knew I had to finish this, if I wanted to grow as a person. I set a six month plan where I would check off important goals I had been unable to achieve in the chaos that was my life in Glasgow. I wanted to pass my driving test, find a flat I could afford by myself, pass the course and complete my PT qualifications. It didn't take me long to find a local flat I could afford. I had been paying far too much for the flat in Glasgow due to its location so it was almost saving me money. The town was of course nothing like Glasgow but it benefitted me in that I had no distractions, my friends were mostly in Glasgow and it made me appreciate them when I did see them. It was more of an event than just casual drinking in my flat. We went to concerts, met up for birthdays and spontaneous days off we had together and if anything our relationships grew from it. Having my mum 10 minutes away was nothing to turn my nose up at either, not only could I discuss at length the course and pick at her years of experience, she also suggested books I could read to further my learning and I took them all on board. It had become my obsession to understand my mind better and learn from it. It's part of the motivation behind me writing this and I thank her every time the course is brought up as I feel it definitely changed my life for the best.

By unit three we had been introduced to other theories such as the psychodynamic perspective and cognitive behavioural therapy. I feel this is where the course was taken to a new level. There was a lot of information on both subjects in the beginning but rather than being overwhelmed by this I found myself more engaged and interested to learn more. I think with CBT and psychoanalysis being more structured and challenging to the counsellor, in my opinion, it suited my personal thought process better than person centred. Due to the nature of seeing the emotion almost as a result of certain thoughts or behaviours and offering more ways to trace where the feelings were coming from. In my own life having this as a way to break down my thought process to reveal how I was really feeling became a super power. It was so common for me to feel something and just let it sit there and build as I didn't know what to do with it. Now I was able to work backwards in my mind to get to the root feeling and ultimately see where it was coming from. I faced a great deal of embarrassment moving back home, I was afraid of what people might think of me, that I had failed. I really had to ask myself what was more important. What I thought of me or what I thought everyone else thought of me. The brutal reality of it is, no one's thinking about you. People are so engrossed in how things affect them, half of them wouldn't even notice I'd moved home if I never pointed it out. Coming to terms with my own short comings and using them as fuel to better myself left little time for any self-pity or guilt. I was working in a place that gave me no pride, which I was embarrassed to be in. But I had my goals set and I knew it was only temporary. If I learnt to deal with the setback positively it would be a useful skill to have for the rest of my life, I grew confidence from staying focused on where I was going, not where I was. Remarkably my previous detest of authority was forgotten, I found myself seeking out people with experience like my mum and implemented what they said. To be smart with my money, and not let my ego make decisions for me.

Money was tight as I was so used to having expendable funds each month. My work was in an awkward place to get to with public transport and it resulted in me having to cycle 5 miles every day before work and back. I used the gym at the hotel on my break to get a workout in and my evenings were spent reading and studying for my last module of the course. My days off were routine as I didn't really have much money to spend on enjoying myself. I would get lonely in the flat myself and it grew a string of relationships that never really lead anywhere. I was too focused on trying to improve myself that when it got to a stage where the relationship needed more attention I would back off. It was a narcissistic way to live and I knew that but I wanted the comfort of having someone there with me, I missed the affection previously shared with my ex-girlfriend. I wasn't getting into a relationship until I had worked on myself.Call it selfish I could agree but I had spent the last three years working and avoiding what I truly wanted, I had to do it now.

My course had only 4 weeks left. It became all-consuming for me. Our practice had lead us to longer counselling sessions where we were asked to bring something real. It was the first time I had said a lot of this out loud and the profound impact, I realised it had all had on me, took me by surprise. I remember not knowing where to start. I felt like a broken record speaking about my dad and then my relationship, and the unfairness of the chef's actions. It didn't control me anymore. I had felt every possible feeling there was connected to them that the impact was lessened. I had closed a big part of my life that was always painful to think of. I had got to the end of the tunnel, it hurt that my dad and my ex-girlfriend couldn't come with me. This I had learned, if you want genuine relationships and love in your life you need to risk being vulnerable and getting hurt. It was therapy in every sense of the word for me and I had gained strength from facing everything that I thought made me weak. From the list of books my mum had gave me at the start of my learning, one in particular took lead. She suggested a book that would inspire great growth with Balanced Dreamers and myself, It was Brene' Browns, Daring Greatly. The book is from a lifetime worth of research into vulnerability and shame. She masterfully offers a thought process around vulnerability, in how anything worth doing or feeling or having has a level of vulnerability to it. To love something opens you up to being hurt by that, you give apart of yourself to that person or thing that you surrender full control in trusting them to love you back and protect your feelings. To act in a way that faced great vulnerability actually displayed real bravery. A lot of my research and teachings around this book were documented on my website, it launched a completely new lifestyle approach for me and I would encourage you to read the book. I had asked the universe to let me experience vulnerability and in the short span of reading the book I had lost my job in Glasgow, went through a horrible break up, faced my own perception of failure from moving back to my mums and my finances had plummeted to the point I was barely scraping by. I'm sure you will have heard the saying before, where there is discomfort there is often growth. This had never been truer for me. I gave everything I could to the course and I had passed. It is my proudest achievement to date, from getting almost useless exam results, to now having a certificate in psychotherapy gave me great pride. A month later I would finally pass my level 2 personal training qualifications and eventually my driving test as well. I had achieved all the goals I had set out to get at the start of the year and I allowed myself to enjoy it. Not only did I have more free time I had the opportunity to make more money with these new qualification. I was truly happy again for the first time in what felt like years.

As the weeks went on the settling feeling from finishing all my goals left me with nothing immediate to work on. I noticed that not much had really changed from my day to day world. I still had to work in a kitchen, I hated, just to afford my flat. There was no clear way forward for me and my mood started to slip back to disappointment and depression. I thought I had done enough to change my life but the more I found myself chasing the next pay check, I could feel my loss of motivation. I went back to watching the entrepreneurs I followed, they had been a big motivator for me finishing the course. Gaining the ability to communicate with people would surely benefit me if I was to start a business and live a life like they had. I now spent my time learning business, what did I need to know and how to get there. I came to the basic understanding that you can't be in business without selling, marketing and product. Despite what the product is I had to be able to sell it and market it properly so its value was displayed appropriately. This opened up a line of communication between me and my ex-girlfriend.We were still civil with each other the majority of the time. Her circumstances had changed to where she now worked in marketing for a big radio station and I asked her all I could about building a following for Balanced Dreamers. I didn't feel embarrassed to ask for help anymore my ego had all but diminished. I realised if I was going to move forward in life I couldn't just act as if I knew what I was doing and actually learn how. It was time to walk before I could run, finally. As much as I learned about marketing and the best time to post and target specific audiences and properly create a brand image it all boiled down to consistency. If I was only posting once a week it wasn't enough, and ultimately I knew that. The thing was I didn't feel comfortable putting myself out there, I wasn't particularly confident anymore, I no longer trusted I was good at anything. Being outgoing through social media just didn't feel true to me, despite this I filmed some videos and took some pictures with little response. My value to me lay in what I could say, what I would write down for people to take their own teachings from. That's where I felt confident so that's where I put most of my efforts. I started writing blogs for Balanced which in all honesty has lead me to this book.

I knew I was now wasting time in the kitchen, I had no desire to go back to a senior role and knew the longer I stayed the harder it would be for me to progress anywhere else. I was about to turn 24 and I felt like I had done nothing with my life. I knew a lot in theory but I didn't practice what I preached. For the fourth time in my life I would walk out of a job, it felt so familiar to me that I stayed quiet even in my own mind. Despite them phoning me to go back and offering me more money I knew if I didn't leave now I would regret it later in life. Regret is my biggest fear in life, I feel physically sick at the thought of not living up to my potential. I have this nightmare of this old man at a bus stop, having done nothing meaningful with his life,he starts to cry uncontrollably and it's like no one can see him. I realise this is a fear I have and that I see myself in him. This keeps me moving forward. Fear is optional it can be ignored and it can be used as fuel. I had this sense of impending doom if I didn't keep improving anywhere I could. I also developed the opposite of that to give me positive motivation. I went back to my law of attraction teachings again and envisioned a life like that of the entrepreneurs I looked upto. Working for myself, standing for something having a purpose to life that was bigger than myself. I also had material goals I wanted to achieve but they didn't have the same impact for me. I told myself in these moments that every decision would be made towards this ideal I had created and away from the old man crying at a bus stop. It was a technique I had learned from listening to Jordan Peterson talk. He explained it as creating your own heaven and hell, and that to get to heaven and avoid hell you had to make all your decisions knowing that each descision could lead you to either destination. It is an intense way to exercise control of yourself and can cause uncertainty and guilt quite easily. But for a short period of time it starts to build momentum, you no longer question what you should do. Therefore less time feeling guilty when you choose to ignore your responsibilities, you make more conscious decisions.

I knew I needed to get into sales, marketing didn't come naturally for me but I thought with my training in communication I would be at an advantage for sales. Everything I had learnt about sales had been consistent with communication, the body language, awareness of the other person's tone and word choices. Knowing the psychology behind the impulse to buy and the behaviours around people's decision making. That people would follow a crowd if they weren't sure so you would emphasise the popularity of what you were selling. Building trust through appearing unbiased, keeping the salesmanship subtle planting a seed that makes them think it was all their idea.This is very similar to CBT counselling approaches. I felt confident I could grasp it well and improve my career path. The trouble with getting a decent sales job is everyone wants you to have experience. When it came to high commission earning salesmen and women they were only as good as their previous numbers. I had no experience in sales so to improve my c.v. I exaggerated about my PT and how I had developed sales techniques from getting clients, little did they know I hadn't trained a single client that wasn't family or friends. Despite this I got many rejections from my applications. I received only one interview offer and jumped at the chance. I didn't even read into what the job entailed or what I would be selling but it was a step in the direction I wanted. Because of my lack of knowledge on the job I directed the interview towards general sales basics that I had learned and really tried to impress the boss with my own communication skills within the interview. We spoke briefly on the physical training I supported, as he was an avid gym goer and he complimented me on being able to speak as if I was older than my years. I had left the interview feeling confident and within half an hour they had phoned to offer me a second interview. Still I had no understanding of the role and even the company's website had been vague in its structure, but I had committed to sales and this was the only door opening for me. The second part of the interview was with a younger employee, he explained that if offered the job, I would be in his team. As he continued with his explanation of the role he told me it would be residential sales. I'm being honest here I thought he meant real estate when he first said that. But to my disappointment he explained that we would be going door to door to get people to change their energy suppliers to our clients. Most of me stopped listening when he said this, now I knew why the website had been so vague. I would have never applied if I had known it would be this. He broke down the commission structure and explained that as you move up you could earn more and really painted an achievable attractive income. I was aware he was however a salesman and anything he said would be taken with a pinch of salt. It was the most obvious pyramid scheme I had ever seen, even the company logo had a pyramid on the website. Basically the more we earned ourselves the company would earn nearly 50x more for every sale. I was annoyed after the interview I felt as though I had wasted my time and almost panicked into taking another chef job. It was on a call to my ex-girlfriend that this turned around.

We had spoken on and off since moving apart and she was still a calming voice for me during this time, we had helped each other even after the break up and she had even moved in for a few weeks to get a break from her family. She had offered to say to her mum in the past about getting me a job with the company she worked for. I had declined the offer due to my pride, I was embarrassed to take the hand out. It threatened my ego around taking care of myself. Foolishly on my part I had been this way in the past and it was my natural reaction to feel judged and looked after. Now though I needed her help, I swallowed any pride I had left and asked her to set up an interview. I knew even if I was successful in getting the job, it would be months before I would physically start the job. So I also took the job as a door to door salesman despite every fibre of my being telling me it would be horrible. The same night I had phoned my close friend and asked about his job, at the time he was working with a chef agency and I remembered him speaking highly of the job. I applied to be on the agency list as a chef until I was on my feet. This allowed me to pick up shifts so I could keep the roof over my head till I found my feet. I was surprised how quickly things had come together, it was all at once, just like when things went bad it wasn't just one thing but multiple.

Thankfully after my ex's mum had phoned for me my interview was only a couple days later. I applied the same approach from the interview earlier in the week. I realised that the universe had given me a warm up interview before the big one. The pressure I felt around the interview crippled me into severe anxiety, I had to phone my mum almost in tears before I left the house. I knew about anxiety and where it was coming from and how to compart mentalise a thought pattern down to its bearable factors but nothing was working for me. My head was spinning with thoughts like, what if I'm asked something I don't know? What if I let my ex's mum down after she had helped me? What if I blow it and end up back in the kitchen full time? How am I going to pay my rent? Will I need to move back in with my mum again? What a failure I'd be! What is wrong with you! You have to get this! I was so relieved when my mum finally answered the phone that I couldn't get my words out. After me frantically throwing word vomit through the phone she had grasped how I was feeling and started to talk. I have the utmost admiration to anyone who masters the art of calming someone down the way my mum did. She asked me to think about her dog Sam. Sam had been in our family for 5 years now, he was the most placid gentle little Jack Russel anyone could ever meet. I loved the very bones of him and during my depth of depression and grief he had been a welcomed escape from the inside of my head. I had woke up from nightmares of seeing my dad dying a few times while staying at my mums house and crept down to the kitchen to give him a hug. My mum then asked me how I feel when I think about Sam. I said that I felt calm around him and in the moment, when I see him playing or being cute. She then asked me to locate where in my body I felt this feeling, having done the counselling course I knew what she meant by this. I told her that I felt it high in my chest and that it was a comforting feeling. My mum continued to say that if I was ever feeling anxious that thinking of something as joyous as a pet and then focusing your breathing and energy towards that feeling it would help take you away from the anxiety. To some this might not have worked and I don't claim it to be a miracle breakthrough in anxiety research, but it had a powerful effect on me and I went into the interview much more calm and in control than I had felt only hours before. The conversation with the boss at the branch was over in five minutes, I had been offered the job and I would start in 6 weeks' time. I felt silly having been so anxious before it after seeing how easy it went. Again showing me the real power of emotions and how understanding and feeling them is so important.

The gap between now and the new job was still a month and a halfs rent away so the next day I started the door to door selling. The morning before we went out to chap doors was always a sales meeting. I'm sure some of you will have worked in a sales environment before and may be familiar with this but to me it was like theatre class at school. I walked into a loud busy room with no tables or chairs, everyone was facing each other going over their sales routine. It was both bizarre and intriguing to me having come from a busy kitchen it was completely foreign to me. I immediately enjoyed it, the sheer simplicity of the job at first hand felt almost fake. The deal we were selling was a no brainer, we were saving people money and costing them nothing to change I thought it was going to be easy money. It took me all of an hour to realise it wasn't going to be easy, it was hard. It was difficult enough trying to get people not to slam the door on you, never mind get bank details and explain the product. I wanted to quit, I was starting that new job anyway I could survive until then I thought. I was so embarrassed chapping strangers doors to try and ask for money it felt like begging. I stopped myself though. I thought if this is only temporary why not get the most out of it, while I can. It became a right of passage for me, if some of those successful entrepreneurs had got their start here then why not me. I paid attention the following days and really tried to learn the way the high paid employees sold. The best salesmen in my team was also the best in the room. He was a few years older than me but he had tattoos and went to the gym just like me. I annoyed him for every tip and trick he could offer and we became genuine friends. He had explained he also ran a food truck with food inspired from his travels and that I should go help him at his next festival in the coming weeks. I agreed to help if he helped me get better at sales and we spent time talking about his approach. I came to find out he was doing it almost completely instinctively and it was almost impossible to mirror, but he was someone to look up to and I had made a real friend in him. I struggled on with what I had learned and ended the week with a few sales. I had made £120 for a week's work. This was brutal but it was as my favourite entrepreneurs would say, character building. The next week I went into fresh, knowing what to expect and choosing to stay positive as I could. I used it as a test, if I could stay confident with the rejections and even smile through it, it would indeed strengthen my character. The sales started to come gradually, I genuinely started to really enjoy it. My pre judgements had been wrong, I spent most of the day talking to people most of which were at least polite in their rejections. Any social anxiety I was holding onto from a teenager left me after only a couple of days. The days were still hard, especially if I didn't get a sale and I was thankful to have the other job to look forward to. In fact if I hadn't had that job set up I would probably not have done it, and all the growth from the discomfort of chapping strangers doors wouldn't have happened. Funny how life works out sometimes.

At home I had my ex-girlfriend staying whenever it suited her. Our relationship now had proved we had changed as people since breaking up it was not like before. We fought for the final time over her treating my house like a hotel. She would leave it a mess and stay out for days, coming home drunk and looking rough. I genuinely cared for her and was trying to look out for her but she saw it as me being highly strung and ignored my concerns. I had let how I felt about her blind me from what had been happening, she had been using me for somewhere to live and she was now moving out. I said my final goodbyes to her and the pain we'd caused each other over the years. I didn't care about being single now, no one was better than someone who didn't respect me. Things we had opened up about to each other in our vulnerable little bubble, were now being used as weapons in our argument.

It had went from the deepest form of love I had ever known, to a genuine hatred for one another. I had gotten used to the feeling of having lost her before, this just made it easier. I told myself that I would never go back and we still haven't properly spoken since. I linger sometimes going back and forth all day with the memories we have together and depending on the ones I choose to think of, paint a completely different picture from the actual relationship. It had monumental highs and equally devastating lows but like everything in my life I find most peace from it when I think of it as being balanced. It was everything it needed to be, hopefully for the both of us, everything happens for a reason.

The following week I was pleased to be busy again. I was working with my friend in his food truck through in Edinburgh and this meant long eventful days. I felt comfortable in the portable kitchen although it was like nothing I had worked in before. I had the experience in cooking that he didn't have, and he had the experience in sales I didn't have. Between us we drummed up business and talked to hundreds of people over the weekend. The festival didn't live up to his expectations however and as the first day came to a close he realised he had under estimated the profit margin. To break even we would have to sell a lot in the following days even with our best salesmanship it didn't look likely. I knew that I probably wasn't going to make any real money from this weekend and although I needed it more than ever I decided to go and help anyway. I was enjoying talking with him during the quiet times of the day, he told me about similar stories from his past that made us understand each other better. He told me of his travels and we spoke about that feeling, we both agreed we had searched for. That feeling as if something is missing. He explained that from his travels he had felt, finally, satisfied and encouraged to be himself from the world around him. This made me want to travel to feel this for myself. He spoke in a way that resonated with me, I could see similarities in myself and he made me feel confident about my future. I would later meet up with him and he's still the same ambitious hard working guy, I aspire to be like. We laughed about the fact we made no money from the weekend we worked together after spending most of it on beer on the final night.

I had scrapped my way closer to my start date with my upcoming job. I had taken the opportunity from the agency to go work for a week and live in the hotel as I worked. At the time I was desperate for money and this one week of work would pay me enough to pay my rent and support myself until my new job. I had fought against the idea of going back to a kitchen like this. I had a fear of getting stuck there again, but I knew it would get me through. I was relieved to get the break away, albeit for work. The hotel was on an island in the highlands where people visited to go hill walking in the summer and most of the businesses were seasonal. It was quiet and peaceful. I found I was working with chefs who worked the season almost nonstop before taking a few weeks off to recover, oddly reminiscent of how I would work only stopping when I'd burned out. The work itself didn't faze me like I thought it would, not a lot of kitchens made me feel unprepared after the pressure of being sous in the restaurants in Glasgow. As much as I was proud of my ability it was another reminder of just how hard I had been working for my living. This had been my first full week in a kitchen for two months and I had to admit I missed the buzz. There's something enjoyable to me of being constantly busy. It makes me feel like I'm capable of more, the adrenaline high of a busy service had always been confidence building, satisfaction daily from getting through the chaos. Although not an easy profession to keep at a high level. By the end of the week I felt as though I'd always been there, my day was Spartan like. I slept in the staff accommodation on an unbearably firm wooden bunk bed, in the morning I would get up a few hours before my shift and walk along the beach and watch the boats to clear my head. There's something freeing about being in a completely different environment, I had a lot to think about in that short week there. I found peace from my relationship with my ex, I finally allowed myself a pat on the back for trusting myself. I had taken another leap of faith leaving the kitchen full time and I felt rewarded by the job I had to look forward to and having the outlet of being a chef as a support to get there. Without getting caught up in the inevitable politics that run deep in a restaurant, I was just visiting, which made the whole experience much more enjoyable. I felt as if I had been through the worst, I had went nearly four months without a proper wage. I still managed to pay for my flat and feed myself. I thought if this is as bad as it gets, I'm no longer scared of the future.

On the ferry home I had a lot to look forward to. It was my friend's birthday and I was heading straight to his for a party and to see my friends. My brother was due to be married the following month, I was due to start my new job the following week and the money I had just made would fund it all. I allowed myself to enjoy it. My immediate future looked bright and I eased into the optimism it brought me. It's often the small things in life right after hardships that bring the highest joy for me. I realise that perhaps I almost create more struggle sometimes, I look for the hard way to get somewhere as if that would make me feel worthy of the rewards. It served me well for the most part as it drove me to push forward as I left myself no choice. Having burnt bridges in the past, but I was now aware that maybe there had been an easier way all along, that I had ignored. That was something to think about going forward, for now it was spending time with my friends for his birthday. A full day spent in the sun with his family celebrating his 21st it was one of our fondest memories as a group and it had come at the perfect time. It would be this evening that a relationship for me would spark from being introduced to a mutual friend. I still wasn't looking for a relationship and she agreed that neither was she, everything seemed to be falling into place effortlessly. It can feel that way sometimes, equally when things go bad it feels like everything happens at once and your world collapses. I don't know why but for me it makes sense, again the law of attraction teachings came to mind, with my change in focus and energy I would be misled to think it wouldn't naturally effect everything. The saying "its not about waiting for the storm to pass, it's about learning to dance in the rain" rings profound here. Often when changes are happening everywhere and you feel lost in the middle, the outcome can really be determined by your reactions to it. The more things changed in my life, I learned to just let them, all the energy spent wishing and stressing for it to be better slows down the process. I continue to practice this relaxed approach to changes but it's not always black and white. It is normal to plan and envision a life you want but the more detailed your expectations the more you can stop a manifestation in its tracks. The most exciting and joyous times of my life have come almost immediately after anxiety and uncertainty of the outcome.

The day had finally come to start my new job. I would spend a week getting to know everyone before going to training for a week externally. The two people I would be working immediately with were lovely, they made me feel welcome and spoke to me honestly about the role. They explained that it really wasn't that hard a job and that as long as you done what was asked it paid well and there was no pressure. Having come from a chef background I thought they were joking. There was no immediate jobs to complete every day, it was the most laid back position I could have created. I was confused, did every job, other than chefs, this easy? As the weeks passed I found it hard to keep busy and get used to the change of pace from what I was used to. There was a lot of information to digest but the literal implications of that knowledge were not consistent I would maybe only use that knowledge a few times a day dependant on the client. The external training confirmed my co-workers description of the role, it was over three days spent doing ice breakers and nonsense tasks to fill out the simplicity of the role. I didn't know if I was going to last here, if I'm honest, I wanted to work hard, it was the only pace I knew. It dawned on me that this wasn't a bad thing, this was an opportunity. The energy I had every day because I hadn't worked so hard was useful, I could train as much as I wanted and I could finally focus on finishing level 3 of my personal training qualifications. It brought a balance back to my life. I didn't even realise was off, I could look after myself properly and avoid burning out.

I had time to stay on top of housework and see some day light through the week. A luxury not readily available in a kitchen believe it or not.

I found traction pretty quickly, I would start work earlier than I did in the kitchen but I would finish earlier too. I went to the gym in the evenings and went home to study. I now had the time to do all these things without having to be up all night. I developed the routine to the point I finished level 3 within a few weeks having put it off for almost two years, and reignited my passion for helping others. After a month of working for the company I had also bought my first car it had been a long time coming for me as my lessons and tests were sporadic, due to me moving home multiple times and having a broken stream of income. I used to daydream about having a car, every day on the long bus and train rides to where ever I was working. It made long days even longer having to wait for buses and trains to get home. The car type, size colour wasn't important, I love cars but the ones I really want are a while away still. I bought an 8 year old Volkswagen polo, it had only done remarkably, little miles for its age and it was more than affordable for me. I was stopped in my tracks when I finally sat in it for the first time. The old me would of turned my nose up at it, due to egotistical beliefs. I had grown to the point it no longer bothered me what others thought, I had a home and a car I had achieved this by myself. With no hand outs and after years of struggling to stay on my own two feet. The fact I could now freely go visit my friends and get to work under my own steam was freedom I will never take for granted. I try and stop myself when I compare it to bigger and better cars. The reality is there will always be something to work towards, but if you don't enjoy what you have now, you don't get to enjoy the journey.Which is the longest part. I also wrote more consistently for balanced and the majority of that work is still used today. I had time to spend time on developing my ideas and expressing them through writing, it was for a bigger purpose. My blogs will probably always be free I take pleasure in doing something for others. I also developed the relationship with the girl I'd started speaking to at the 21st party. She would stay after work a couple nights through the week and we took things slow. I didn't want a relationship with her and I made it clear from the beginning. It wasn't that there was anything wrong with her ,on the contrary, but I just wanted to focus on my own development and the business. I felt like we were on the same page and it was a laid back vibe I appreciated her and enjoyed the break from the work I was putting in. At work I had settled into my position and had a group of boys the similar age as me that grew into genuine friendships. They were ambitious like me, hence the salesman role. We spoke about business and cars and all things that we were focused on achieving. We agreed the outlook of life from a social media perspective didn't interest us. There was no need to flaunt materialistic goods, to us it just showed a lack of maturity. I was inspired by our conversations and this made me proud of the work I had been doing for Balanced, pleased that I wasn't the only one who seen through the shallowness of social media. It was here of all places that I would pick up an old habit I thought I had finished with.

The more goals I set in front of me the more I would feel overwhelmed into procrastination. If I didn't get enough done that day I felt guilty and if I sat there for too long it would slip into depression. It made me feel like I'd taken what I had for granted. Every day I had to move forward somehow or I felt I was going to explode. The same pressures I felt with my dad, around rushing to get in a position I could support him, were there stronger than ever but with no clear direction of where to put this energy. To slow myself down I turned back to smoking weed. In my time of abstinence from the weed there had been some more research around it had developed.It seemed almost like a feasible tool for a lot of the world, the highly successful and average Joe alike. It was proven to reduce inflammation and corsitol production, the stress hormone, it also debunked a lot of the mental health implications that used to be stigma around it, there was infact no correlation between smoking and psycosis and other mental health defects. The people I looked up to who smoked it did so with the understanding of balance and moderation with it. Along with a healthy lifestyle they were able to use it as a positive tool to relax and brainstorm without having negative health reprecussions. I would smoke on days I wasn't working and it would allow my mind to quiet just enough to know what to do next. I got a lot of my writing done while being somewhat high. I knew if I could control my intake of it that it wouldn't have any adverse effects on me and it's something I still use today. I don't flaunt it around or make it known that I partake but with my friends from work on occasion we would sit in my flat and smoke. It was so much better than alcohol for me, I had no dip into depression the following day. It seems to benefit me but I will continue to be cautious and monitor my habit as I know it doesn't take long for me to become addicted to things. This is in no way a recommendation to smoke, this book isn't what to do and what not to, this is just my experiences and views around my own growth, take from it what you will and if you think I'm reckless or ignorant from my statements, then no love lost. I no longer let other people's opinions of me change my opinions.

Along with new positive relationships, like everywhere there were some people I just couldn't see any good in as much as I wanted to. I have addressed this in a blog on BD and I need to be careful not to point any direct fingers, but the sales environment has some of the most selfish, miserable, materialistic people I have ever met. No amount of money or status seemed like it was going to make these people happy, yet all they spent their time doing was chasing more status and money. Engulfed by material gain. I understand fully the fact that it's their livelihood and how they live but from my perspective it looked like a shallow empty existence. I knew money didn't make me happy in itself I needed the bigger motivation, a higher purpose. This back and forth of extremes everyday caused me to focus more than ever on what I really wanted to do with my life. I told myself that regardless of how much I make financially the source of it had to be something I genuinely stood for or that could at the very least support that. As much as the nice cars and houses excite me the void in my soul from not following my dreams would never be filled by anything less than purpose. I've been known to be an intense individual but I make no apologies for it, perhaps having read so far you get a better understanding of me but it doesn't really matter, to me, if you don't. My time spent trying to convince others and fit in are long gone. I owe it to myself and the people I love to focus on what is meaningful to me. As I hope they do the same. I didn't let these people bother me or effect my mood, I knew whatever caused their attitude had nothing to do with me and I stayed with the hard working humble group I had.

As if to put a cherry on top of my year my brother would be married to the love of his life in a beautiful ceremony the following month. It was an emotional day to say the least. It meant meeting for the first time since my dad passing his side of the family. My dad's sister and my cousin who had cut all ties with us until it suited her. My dad's twin brother had chosen not to come not that we were surprised by this. My resentment was consoled by remembering it was my brother's decision to invite them and I would be civil for his sake. After speaking briefly with some family members I realised that it didn't matter how I felt about them. I had to accept, if I wasn't perfect and made mistakes and could act selfishly in the past that they were no different. I forgave them for everything and felt the weight leave my shoulders. As the day continued it was getting closer and closer to my speech. I was my brothers' best man and I wanted to give the best speech I possibly could. I wrote what I felt had to be said, with my dad not being there I wanted to express that he would have been proud of him and that I wanted to thank my brother for being my support and role model through the years. I wanted to welcome his wife into our family and tell her I had already seen her as a sister. I built it up so much in my head that when I was finally passed the microphone the emotion just poured out of me. I managed a version of the speech I had written but it was disappointing from what I had planned. The embarrassment I expected to follow from showing emotion in front of everyone there, never came. Through the counselling course, my teachings around vulnerability and the complete detrementation of my ego in all the ways I had to swallow my pride over the years allowed me to just accept what had happened. It was therapeutic to be so vulnerable in front of others and actually come out stronger from it. I enjoyed the day from that point onwards, I danced with my mum and welcomed her husband as a father figure after all those years he had looked out for us and my mum. I loved him like family. It was a very happy time and made all the more enjoyable knowing that only two years earlier we had been at the funeral of my dad. My best friend was my plus one, he had been there through the worst times with me it felt right to have him there for a celebration.

With work keeping my finances stable and having enough to enjoy every month my procrastination had got worse. I wasn't smoking weed all day before anyone jumps to conclusions. I had nothing concrete to look forward to, no immediate goal again. Work commitments from my friends meant seeing them wasn't as frequent as in the past. When we finally met up it was like all this pent up frustrations would boil over resulting in me drinking again. Not just socially to enjoy the company but as if I was trying to get somewhere with it. I would drink till I blacked out and wake up in a depth of depression again. As much as I knew I was causing it, it didn't seem to stop me. The feeling of complacency set my bones on fire. I wanted to be patient and enjoy what was happening for me but a dark twisted part of me wanted the chaos. Wanted the struggle, it was the only time I felt alive. When things were going too easy I would be drawn to thinking of the bad stuff. My dad dying replayed over and over in my mind till I had to do something.

It was during this time the girl I had been casually seeing told me she was pregnant. To say I was heartbroken by this was an understatement. We had spoken about this at the start, that we didn't want any children for a long time. She told me she had been on birth control, so I was shocked as you can imagine. My first response was anger, she had used me and lied to me. She explained that she had a condition that meant she wasn't supposed to be able to have kids and this might be her only chance. I felt physically sick for days. I had always imagined my first child being with someone I loved and wanted to be with. I felt like she had robbed me of that experience. I know I'm probably not going to win any fans from young mothers saying this but it's what was profound in my mind. As time went on and her bump grew the more I wanted a way out. I had tried my best to empathise with her situation and didn't want to be overly cruel to someone I did care about, but I hated her for going against our agreement at the start of the realtionship. I didn't want a baby let alone one with someone I wasn't in love with. I don't mean to paint her in a bad light and having spent enough time with her I see she is a genuine person dispite being somewhat immature. She is also absolutely gorgeous, my son will be a handsome young man if hes anything like his mother but it doesn't change how I feel. In a sense I don't want to let myself love her, I don't want it right now. I spent so long deeply in love with my ex that it feels comfortable not to have that vulnerability. It may not make sense to some people but it's what's true for me in this moment. It caused an internal fight within me about what I was going to do. My male ego told me to stand up and take responsibility but every fibre of my being was shouting run. Since then my relationship with her is almost non-existent, my son is due in August and I still don't know what role I want to have in his life. It's the single most powerful thing I've ever faced, no matter what I do I know people will have their opinions, and that's okay. They don't need to live my life, I do. I know deep down that it will be everything it was supposed to be. Maybe having someone other than myself to work hard for will push me to new heights. Again I have a choice, to torture myself over what's happening or face it calmly with as much confidence as I can muster. I know which one is easier.

       I was in the best shape of my life at this point, the gym was the only positive output for how I was feeling. The more I improved the more the goal posts moved. I fell out of the idea of being a PT everyone I knew that was doing it was pedalling the same shit. They have been for years. The urge to say something about it flew out of me in several raw blogs.Not understanding why people were lying or masking the truth about physical and mental health. They promoted quick fixes and fad diets, as someone who has spent the majority of their lives researching and studying health from a holistic perspective, I promise you its all bullshit. You have to find what works for you but not only that you need to know why it works for you, it takes time and consistency and hard unforgiving self-work. But the reality doesn't sell as well as six minute abs. I felt exhausted, where was I going to feel happy and content in life, I asked myself continuously. It was not from a place of depression or sadness but from anger, from frustration, from not feeling seen or heard in my life. This grew to a point I felt like giving up, I had spent nearly four years building Balanced as best I could. I had looked at myself from every angle and tried to improve even in the most desperate areas. It all seemed pointless.

I had built up expectations for everything that I wanted from life and this lead to comparing everything with that. I was never going to be satisfied with this mind-set and working harder wasn't the answer. I gave in. I didn't give up but I gave in. I gave in to trying to have all the answers and knowing what to do. I trusted that life would carve a path for me anyway, like it had always done. I knew genuine happiness for me came from putting time into Balanced, whatever that manifested as, writing, podcasts, videos even research, regardless of the support and funds it gave me. I focused on what I could control, I didn't commit to anything I wasn't completely sold by. It took time, it happened gradually. The years of learning the theory behind thoughts and emotions was not the same as actually feeling them and allowing them to guide me. It wasn't a fight or a struggle that I had been preparing for but more like a cleansing. I stripped back everything I had gone through. I compartmentalised it using what I had learnt about psychology from the counselling course through meditation and writing I got it all out. Spending time deliberately in the uncomfortable feelings from my past and finding peace from them. Understanding that everything had been necessary to get me to here. I realised that the only thing that had caused any change in life was the feelings I had towards the situation. My emotions had been guiding me all along, I just had to trust them, over all else. There's a deeper belief just behind the self doubt that whispers to me in times of struggle. I've never attempted to put this into words as I feel it risks jepordising the value in the process to get here. I believe everything is energy, that that energy is what makes me, me. My soul or higher consciousness or god or whatever you want to call it is energy. Therefore if that energy was all knowing and infinately wise then at some point, way before I was even born. I must have known what this existance would bring me. I must of seen the future and decided to come into this body. I must then have everything I need to live the life I'm supposed to, to face and adapt from all the pressures and obstacles put in my way. A complete belief that I'm exactly everything I'm supposed to be and will become. Take from that what you will, it gets hard to accept at times of struggle but it keeps the wind on my back as I continue to move forward.

As I'm writing this it's April of 2020 and the majority of the world is in lock down. People are showing their true colours even more than usual. There's always going to be those who see every situation as an opportunity. There's always going to be people who look out for themselves regardless of how the worlds being effected, and there's going to be those who are scared and waiting for answers before they do anything. You or someone you love could die at any point during this epidemic. I'm due to turn 25 in a couple of months and the future is uncertain and unpromised. To me though it always has been this way, it always has been uncertain.

If you're waiting for some revelation, a sentence that sums up life and our meaning for being I don't have one. Balanced Dreamer is how I describe myself, life for me always seemed to balance out one way or another. My friendships, finances, work load, happiness, stress, everything. For every bad day I have now, where I don't feel proud of myself or worthy of my dreams there's a day that follows, that I feel completely where I need to be. I continue to dream of a future I want to create for myself and my family, and I balance the vision with work. I know that keeping a balance of all things important to me, create the dream, everything I have was once a dream. Throughout the hard times I found any balance I could to keep going, the late night gym sessions, working on myself, the stepping down from my sous responsibilities to focus on the course and better myself. How my fitness and health became such a priority having abused my body with drink and drugs. As I go through the years with you in the book I see how very close I came to being trapped in a negative mind-set and ultimately a brutally harsh existence, by letting my circumstances hold me down. My faith above all else keeps me going when I don't see the light at the end of the tunnel, faith that I am only one man and the world doesn't revolve around me.That I can be affected by the same things anyone else can. But that if I focus on the balance that will always be there I can go through anything. In life people are going to look out for themselves, walk over you and judge you and that's okay. You're going to find yourself facing daunting challenges with no strength to continue but you will. Life will happen to you if you need to be dragged kicking and screaming or if you roll with the punches. Working on your health and shortcomings is perhaps the best expenditure of your energy, but even that doesn't give you a free pass. You never know what's round the corner and for those of you in the trenches right now trust me it will pass. And when the next battle comes you'll be stronger having gone through it. I've learnt that the more I agonise over thoughts and try obscene self-discipline and torment myself mentally the more the bars of self limiting beliefs are reinforced. Equally freedom, ease, clarity and joy are only thoughts away.

I could of wrote this 10 times over and still feel I have more to say, but like my life it doesn't have to be perfect to be what was needed.I never claimed to be perfect, the more I go through life I realise the joy isn't in perfection, its in the journey itself. The good and the bad, the beautiful unpredictable but enevitable balance that underlines the chaos weather your aware of it or not. I am however leaving the doubt and self-sabotage of my past in these pages but I have no doubt the hard days will come again. My focuses are going towards raising my son, the best way I can. Using the experiences I've had in my life to guide him to develop his own outlook on life. If I can support him to a point in where he trusts himself enough to go after what he truly wants from life,with no restraints, and remain humble and genuine through his own process I will have lived up to my expectations.Ultimately though he will be my son but it will be his life, I want him to understand his potential and ability early in life and that I don't have all the answers as much as I wish I did.He will be encouraged to question the norm and make his own beliefs for these lessons have brought me to where I am today. I also want to devote more time and energy to building Balanced Dreamers into something that'll stay long after I'm gone for other people dealing with their own life hurdles. Something I can be proud to be apart of and lead it to constantly increasing heights of impact and success. I want the community to be there for people like myself that needed someone just like my mum. So as many people as possible don't have to go through their painful growth spurts with no one to help them along the way, whatever that means to you. Your struggles and hardships don't need to be understood by others, they can be something that happens to everyone. It's your emotional response that causes the trauma and pain, not the situation itself. Lastly I'm going to show the people who were there for me through the dark times what they mean to me, I'm going to continue to love them and tell them daily. Because you never know when a part of your own heart will leave with someone else. Until we meet again, look after yourselves. Look for balance before progress and never stop dreaming.

AFTERWORD

After a very short labour, Gavin arrived yelling like a banshee, this was to be a sign of things to come.He was a beautiful baby, easy and content a joy to be around. As he grew it became obvious he had a strong will and determination to be who he wanted to be. He dressed himself and chose the clothes he wanted. With strange combinations: one outfit I remember well, a thick green sock was paired with a cotton white one protruding from his sandals. Shorts with an oversized jumper tucked in. A colourful life jacket for the swimming pool pulled over the top and as always a hat, todays was bright yellow. A plastic hard hat, curtesy of a love for Bob the builder. The neighbours would comment with affectionate grins "dressed himself this morning, I see"

He had a great imagination and could disappear to his room for ages, when I investigated I would hear him talking with different accents for each character as he played out a story with his toys. Always accompanied with his beloved Teddy. Thick as thieves they were always together. His first great love. This creative part of him over spilled into wonderful stories later in primary school. As we discovered at his annual report from his primary school teacher. She said she had been surprised at the extent of his vocabulary and had questioned his knowledge of understanding the words he used. However she had been surprised that he had used the words with the correct meaning in a new sentence. This teacher a few years after this asked if she could use one of Gavin's stories to help teach her class about descriptive words and grammar points.

One thing that Gavin really struggled with, always, was change any change. Every summer going back to school and a new teacher sent him into a state of panic and distress. It was difficult to understand and to help him with it. This also played out when it came to learning new things.He wanted to ride a horse, I think this came from his love of cowboy movies. However he didn't want to learn he couldn't cope with not being able to do it. He wanted to swim but again didn't want lessons. This went on with all of his activates of which there was many. Even though he struggled and huffed at not quite achieving this the way he imagined he would he never gave up. Stubborn and determined as a primary child this was difficult but do able. As a six foot teenager however almost impossible.

I wanted to hide the stresses and strains of life from my children and the difficulties their dad and I were facing. We had very different views around finances and what was the priority in life. We kept secret our arguments and frustrations maybe too well. I didn't want my children to think badly of their dad or of me. I think when I eventually said I didn't want be married anymore it came as a shock to them if they had seen us argue they might have known it was coming. Hine sight is a wonderful thing. This is the turning point for Gavin he was heartbroken as was I but I couldn't fix it. I was sorry to cause such pain but I would have died if I'd pretended any longer. It was like watching a car crash in slow motion and not being able to change it.

I felt Gavin was stolen from me I couldn't reach him, he wouldn't listen to me. His behaviour deteriorated I didn't recognise him. His anger was all encompassing. I felt that he hated me and even as I tried to hold the boundaries of behaviour and house rules I knew it was a losing battle.His dad and I had very different ideas of how to handle this crisis which became evident when we were called to the school. They had seen a huge change in Gavin as I had too.

His father Alistair had a disliked of authority and obeying the rules, grown out of his treatment by authority in his youth he found it difficult to trust them, I feel this had an influence on how Gavin viewed authority. As a result School didn't get any better.

Gavin had a good, consistent group of friends he was loyal and cared for them. This care and attention was given freely and without question. He was ferociously protective of them and offered support and defence if you were in his group. Unfortunitly his friends did not always offer the same loyalty and support back a lesson Gavin found hard and painful to accept. It confused him why others didn't seem to care as much as he did. He was never short of female friends, girlfriends, I think they were drawn to his gentle understanding and his genuine desire to understand them. He was easy on the eye too. As fitness and looking after his body was becoming more and more important to him. As for the girls I think they felt special, the only one. For Gavin it was just his way of being. I'm sure they got hurt because possibly they believed he only spoke to them in this way but I don't think Gavin realised how seductive and attractive this was to be around. So when things went wrong and Gavin would express his anger people were left feeling hurt and confused. He cared with passion and whole heartedly but he also expressed his anger or hurt with equal force. Some friends, girlfriends and later employers found this difficult to accept or be around.

It's at this point due to his anger over spilling that he decides to join the army. I decide I'm not going to fight his decision I have good reason for this. Don't misunderstand me I do not want my child to join the army but I'm confident it will never happen. Firstly at this moment he is an angry young man he would not listen to anything anybody says. Secondly if we convince him not to join he would always wonder if it was the wrong decision and so we begin the preparation for him joining Clothes are bought and military haircut before off he goes on the plane for his basic training. Second day in I get a phone call.... I want to come home. I am relieved he organises his departure from his army life and heads home.

What now? Culinary collage he excels at this and meets some firm friends too. A job in a high end Glasgow restaurant follows and he settles into the hard working life of a chef with high pressure and long anti-social hours he pushes himself. Any free time is filled with gym and working out. Again he puts his whole heart into his work and the friends he works with. Our relationship is improving he confides in me and asks me to help him work out what's going on for him.

During a holiday in France Gavin called and described how his dad hadn't been himself that day. "Dads not making any sense, he's loaded with the cold". What he was describing to me however sounded like a stroke, but what could I do from so far away I didn't want to panic him, but I knew time was crucial. I recommended that they took him to hospital. After them confirming my fears, things between me and Gavin changed as you would expect. He was struggling to come to terms with the changes in his dad and their conversations were different His dad struggled to find the right words that he meant to say because of damage the stroke had caused. So these conversations were moved to Gavin and I. He had always told me everything eventually sometimes things I didn't want to know. Things my friends found strange that he would tell his mother but I was glad he felt he could tell me. When his dad died the boys rallied round each other and I'm incredibly proud of how they conducted themselves. Their prepared words spoken at his funeral were beautiful and incredibly heart felt. Gavin tried very hard to speak his truth but emotion overwhelmed him and the humanist took over and he had to pause with the emotion it touched in him as he read. His open expression was a surprise to many at the gathering but not me, he had always been open to expressing how he felt and would encourage others to express themselves too.

I think in an effort to control his pain and grief Gavin went back to drinking too much and working too much and doing as many things as possible to keep busy. He was walking about raw and sensitive to everything often quick to anger. There were positives to this over working and promotion came at work although I did feel his head chef/friend was using him a bit. The friends and girls in his life were distracting him more than helping and his home became a bit of a party zone. Where too much booze and whatever else only resulted in him feeling more depressed and morose.

We spoke about this and he knew he wasn't helping himself

it was at this point his relationship was suffering too, we talked about how he could take back his focus and how he could help his communication skills, as he always turned to himself when there was a problem in his life, what could he do to fix things, this is where the counselling skills course began. I knew he'd enjoy it and he'd learn more about himself and what makes him tick. It wasn't long before he could see how his so called friend in the kitchen was using him working ,what seemed like constantly, so he stepped down from the position to look after himself. The chef took this badly and punished him by reducing his wage to minimal. Gavin was hurt and angry at this betrayal so much so he left the very next day, his pride perhaps taking the reins of this decision. He was not unemployed for long and even though everything was changing he kept going.

His relationship was now ended, I'm happy about this she was not right for him. He's in his own flat with a much reduced income, but trying his best to stay optimistic. He continued with his counselling skills course, he learned to drive and he got a new job. I feel this was a great turning point it had been a hard difficult time but he had learned so much about himself. In his independent work with Balanced dreamers he was focusing on vulnerability well he had certainly experienced this in lots of ways all year long.

As he continued to grow and transform into this wonderful sensitive loving young man I'm filled with so much pride. I'm in awe of his gutsy determination to keep going no matter what. Most people facing these challenges would have given up working out and healthy eating seeing these things as unimportant but this discipline gave him strength. When the emotions whirled out of control being physical grounded him and helped him to believe he could do all that he hoped to achieve. Heres to the next wonderful eventful 25 years. Darling.

Printed in Great Britain
by Amazon